THE
Ancient Stone Crosses of Dartmoor
and its Borderland

BY

WILLIAM CROSSING

AUTHOR OF

"*Amid Devonia's Alps,*" "*Tales of the Dartmoor Pixies,*"
"*A Hundred Years on Dartmoor,*" etc.

REVISED EDITION

Illustrated by T. A. Falcon, M.A.

> In many a green and solemn place,
> Girt with the wild hills round,
> The shadow of the Holy Cross,
> Yet sleepeth on the ground.
> RICHARD JOHN KING,
> *The Forest of the Dartmoors.*

Exeter
JAMES G. COMMIN
1902

This scarce antiquarian book is included in our special *Legacy Reprint Series*. In the interest of creating a more extensive selection of rare historical book reprints, we have chosen to reproduce this title even though it may possibly have occasional imperfections such as missing and blurred pages, missing text, poor pictures, markings, dark backgrounds and other reproduction issues beyond our control. Because this work is culturally important, we have made it available as a part of our commitment to protecting, preserving and promoting the world's literature. Thank you for your understanding.

Marchant's Cross.

CONTENTS.

Preface ix

CHAPTER I.
AN OLD WORLD REGION AND ONE OF ITS ANTIQUITIES: Extent of Dartmoor—The Border Towns—Wildness of the Moor—The Forest Perambulations—A home of Ancient Customs—Border Scenery—Antiquities—The Cross an Object of Veneration—Purposes of the Stone Cross—Dartmoor Crosses Rude in Appearance—Their Surroundings—The Border Crosses ... 1

CHAPTER II.
THE BOUNDARY CROSSES OF BRENT MOOR: Brent Hill—Brent Fair—Church of St. Patrick—Christopher Jellinger—Brent Market Cross—Hobajon's Cross—Old Map of Dartmoor—Butterdon Stone Row—Three Barrows—Western Whitaburrow—Petre's Cross—Sir William Petre—Buckland Ford—The Abbots' Way—Clapper Bridge—Huntingdon Cross—The Valley of the Avon 9

CHAPTER III.
BY THE SOUTHERN BORDER HEIGHTS: Ugborough Moor—Bagga's Bush—Old Guide Post—Sandowl Cross—Hookmoor Cross—Ugborough Church—Bishop Prideaux—Owley—Spurrell's Cross—Harford—Broomhill to Ivybridge 22

CHAPTER IV.
FROM THE ERME TO THE PLYM: Ivybridge—The Erme—Church of St. John—Inscribed Stone—Fardle—Blachford—Cornwood—Hawns and Dendles—Cross at Cholwich Town—An Ancient Farmhouse—Blackaton Cross—Cadaford Bridge 29

CHAPTER V.
THE VIA CRUCIS OF THE AUGUSTINE CANONS: Hemerdon Ball—Plympton St. Maurice—Plympton Castle—The Priory—Church of Plympton St. Mary—Cross by the Torry—Browney Cross—Base of Cross at Beatland Corner—Shaugh Cross—Shaugh Church—The White Thorn—The Dewerstone—Cross near Shaden Brake—Cross near Cadaford Bridge—Lynch Down—Marchant's Cross 40

CHAPTER VI.

THE CROSSES OF MEAVY: The Meavy Oak—A Missing Village Cross—Its Discovery and Restoration—Meavy Church—Cross in Wall of Transept—Tomb of Lady Seccombe—Tomb of Walter Mattacott—Gratton—Chapel of St. Matthew—Greenwell Down—Greenwell Girt—Base of a Wayside Cross—Urgles—Wigford Down—An Old Path. 52

CHAPTER VII.

CROSSES ON THE LANDS OF AMICIA, COUNTESS OF DEVON: Bickleigh Vale—Maynstone Cross—Woolwell Cross—Bickleigh Cross—The Church—Socket Stone—Copris Cross—Buckland Abbey—Buckland Monachorum Cross—Shaft of Cross on Crapstone Farm—Horrabridge—Smalacumbe Cross—Sheepstor Cross—A Moorland Church—An Ancient Church House—The Pixies' Cave—The Path of the Monks 57

CHAPTER VIII.

MEAVY TO SAMPFORD SPINEY: Yennadon—Socket Stone at Dousland—Walkampton Church—An Old Church House—Socket-stone—Huckworthy Bridge—Cross on Huckworthy Common—Sampford Spiney Cross—Whitchurch Down 67

CHAPTER IX.

THE ABBOTS' WAY: An Ancient Track—Brock Hill Mire—Red Lake Ford—Broad Rock—Plym Steps—Springs of the Plym—Siward's Cross—Its Early Mention—Inscription on the Cross—Bond mark of the Monks' Moor—Course of the Abbots' Way—The Windypost—Moortown—Cross on Whitchurch Down—Monkeys' Castle—A Broken Wayside Cross—Some Tavistock Worthies 71

CHAPTER X.

A GREEN PATH OF THE MOOR: Buckland to the South-east Border—Crazy Well Pool—Piers Gaveston—A Broken Cross—Remains of Cross by the Wayside—Stone Pillar—Fox Tor—Tomb of Childe the Hunter—A Tradition of the Forest—A Despoiled Monument—Discovery of a Kistvaen—Death of the Lord of Plymstock—Fox Tor Newtake and its Crosses—Crosses of Ter Hill—Stannaburrows—The Down Ridge Crosses—Horse Ford—Horn's Cross—An Old Road—Queen Victoria's Cross at Hexworthy—Holne Moor—Cross in Holne Churchyard—Birthplace of Charles Kingsley—Cross at Hawson—Buckfast Abbey—Base at Ashburton—Cross at Gulwell 84

CHAPTER XI.

FROM THE TAVY TO THE TAW: Tavistock—Old Market Cross—Hermitage of St. John—Inscribed Stones—A Period of Religious Activity—Tavistock Abbey—Remains of Cross at Peter Tavy—

Steven's Grave—Longtimber Tor—Mary Tavy Clam—Mary
Tavy Cross—Forstal Cross—Brent Tor—Lydford—Bra Tor—
Base at Sourton—Cross on Sourton Down—An Ancient
Inscription—Cross formerly at Okehampton—North Lew Cross
—Okehampton Park—Cross at Fitz's Well—Pixy-led Travellers
—Inscribed Stones at Belstone and Sticklepath 108

CHAPTER XII.

AT THE FOOT OF COSDON : Zeal Head Cross—Cross at South Zeal—
Story of John Stanbury—Moon's Cross—South Tawton—
Oxenham Cross—Tradition of the White Bird—Cross at Ring-
hole Copse—Cross at Addiscott—Firestone Ley—Cross at West
Week—An Ancient Border Farmhouse 126

CHAPTER XIII.

THROWLEIGH TO MORETONHAMPSTEAD: Fragments of Crosses at
Throwleigh—An Ancient Base—Restoration of the Cross—
Gidleigh—Murchington—Gidleigh Park and Leigh Bridge—
Cross at Holy Street—Base of Cross at Chagford—Cross at
Way Barton—Surroundings of Chagford—Cross near Cranbrook
—Stone Cross—Week Down—Shorter Cross 132

CHAPTER XIV.

FROM MORETONHAMPSTEAD TO THE WESTERN BORDER COMMONS :
An Old Road—Cross at Lynscott—Headless Cross—Ancient
Guiding Stones—Beetor Cross—A Traditionary Battle—Bennet's
Cross—Heath Stone—Newhouse—Story of the Grey Wethers—
Meripit Hill—Maggie Cross—Jonas Coaker—Cut Lane—The
Lich Path—Clapper Bridges—The Rundle Stone—Long Ash
Hill 140

CHAPTER XV.

CROSSES ON THE BOVEY RIVER: Horse Pit Cross—An Old-time
Village—North Bovey Cross—Cross at Hele—Tradition of a
Chapel by the Stream—Disappearance of the Manaton Cross—
Its Socket-stone—Cross at South Harton Gate—Cross Park—
The Bishop's Stone—Inscribed Stone at Lustleigh—Crosses at
Bovey Tracey—Cross at Sanduck 152

CHAPTER XVI.

WIDECOMBE-IN-THE-MOOR AND THE CROSSES IN ITS NEIGHBOUR-
HOOD : Ilsington—Bag Tor Mill—Cross on Rippon Tor—Cross
in Buckland Churchyard—Wayside Cross at Buckland—Dun-
stone—Cross in Vicarage Garden at Widecombe—Base of Cross
on Widecombe Green—Cross in the Churchyard—Thunder
Storm of 1638—Hameldon and its Barrows—Hameldon Cross
—The Coffin Stone—Dartmeet—Ouldsbroom Cross—Cross
Furzes—Dean Prior—Ancient Track to Plympton—Conclusion. 161

LIST OF ILLUSTRATIONS.

1.	*Marchant's Cross*	*Frontispiece*
2.	*Blackaton Cross*	38
3.	*Shaugh Cross*	47
4.	*Cross on Huckworthy Common*	69
5.	*Cross on Whitchurch Down*	81
6.	*Childe's Tomb*	89
7.	*Cross in Fox Tor Newtake*	96
8.	*Cross near Skir Ford—Down Ridge*	101
9.	*Cross near Horse Ford do.*	101
10.	*Cross on Sourton Down*	119
11.	*Inscribed Stone Sticklepath*	125
12.	*South Zeal Cross*	126
13.	*Cross at Ringhole Copse, South Tawton*	130

PREFACE.

In my former notices of the Stone Crosses of the Dartmoor country, those existing on the moor, and those to be found in the cultivated portions of the border parishes, were dealt with in separate books. In the following pages these two are combined, and much new matter, rendered necessary by the altered state of some of the objects described, has been added. This has required some re-casting, and renders the present in great measure a new book.

Some of the remarks prefixed to my earlier description of the Old Crosses of the Moorlands I venture to repeat here. I stated that my explorations on Dartmoor had extended over many years, and had enabled me to gather much of interest pertaining to its history, its customs, and its objects of antiquity. My researches in that region of tor and stream I have never tired of pursuing, a love for its dear old hills, extending back as far as memory will carry me, attracting me to its wild solitudes, where, by the side of the stone circle and the moss-covered cairn, we seem to stand on the borderland between the present and the distant past.

How much of poetry is there in the memorials of a people who lived on these hills, and who saw the moor as we see it now ages ago. There is truly a rich reward offered to the student of our antiquities, which is denied to those who look with indifference upon the remains of a bygone day. The light shed by the grey stones of the Celt, enables us to read something of the past, and as we advance to historic times, and find the menhir no longer reared upon the heath, and that the circle and the dolmen cease to be upraised, the symbol of that faith which is the salvation of fallen man, rough-hewn from the moorstone block, takes their place, and the lamp is kept brightly burning.

But these memorials which testify to the presence of men who set up by the green paths of the moor the emblem of their religion, have, in many instances yielded to the rude buffetings of the wintry blast, or have been cast down by those in whom, in a later day, these rudely fashioned stones could call up no tender feelings. Too often have I discovered an old cross overturned and partially hidden from view by the heather, its broken shaft and mutilated arms silently upraiding the carelessness that permitted it to remain prostrate on the ground.

To chronicle the existence of such as were previously unknown and to collect evidence, if such might be discovered, respecting the time and purpose of their erection, as well as of those of which mention had been made by others, has been to me a very pleasant and congenial task ; and the happy days spent on the breezy hills of Dartmoor in my search for these relics, which the companionship I enjoyed rendered happier still, will never be forgotten.

These remarks were written some fifteen years ago, and Dartmoor is now to me as ever it was. But previous to their appearance I had made an appeal in behalf of the stone crosses of that old-time region, and it has been a source of gratification to me to find that what little I have done has not been without its effect. Since I first drew attention to these memorials about fifteen of them have been re-erected, and once more are seen by the wayside and in the villages as they were of old. Such evidence respecting the particular purposes they were designed to serve as I could bring together, my knowledge of the topography of the district enabled me the more clearly to read, and to draw the conclusions set forth in these pages, and which in the opinion of a reviewer in *Notes and Queries* are not incorrect.

One of my objects—that of rescuing the wayside and village cross from neglect—has to some extent been accomplished. Another has been the furnishing of a correct description of them, that those who take an interest in these memorials may learn something of their appearance and surroundings, and so far as is possible, of their history; and in this, too, I venture to hope I have not been entirely unsuccessful. While we venerate the cross as a symbol of the Christian religion, it is less that this is so than that it is an object of antiquity that I have called attention to it, and pleaded for its preservation. I should desire that the same care I have asked for the cross should also be bestowed upon the stone remains we usually connect with paganism.

I desire to express my indebtedness to Mr. T. A. Falcon for the pains he has taken in obtaining so fine a series of photographs for the express purpose of illustrating this volume, and for the use of a few which appeared in his book *Dartmoor Illustrated*.

WM. CROSSING.

Black Down, Dartmoor,
 June, 1902.

Via Crucis Via Vera.

The dark'ning shadows filled the vale,
   The way seemed long and drear,
Rough was the track and hard to trace,
   And none to guide was near;
And soon my falt'ring steps were stayed,
   Two paths before me lay,
Oh, for a friendly hand to aid
   And show to me the way!

When lo, a rudely fashioned stone
   From out the gloom appeared,
A moss-grown cross, in days long flown
   By pious hands upreared.
It showed a straight and narrow path—
   No more my steps would stray—
And doubts had ceased to trouble now
   That I had found the way.

'Twas thus when in the wilderness,
   I tried to pierce the gloom,
And find a path to that bright land
   That lies beyond the tomb,
The Promise of the Book shone forth,
   And by its cheering ray
Revealed the Cross of Calvary,
   And then I knew the way.

THE ANCIENT STONE CROSSES OF DARTMOOR & ITS BORDERLAND.

CHAPTER I.

An Old World Region and One of its Antiquities.

Extent of Dartmoor—The Border Towns—Wildness of the Moor—The Forest Perambulations—A home of Ancient Customs—Border Scenery—Antiquities—The Cross an Object of Veneration—Purposes of the Stone Cross—Dartmoor Crosses Rude in Appearance—Their Surroundings—The Border Crosses.

The wild and elevated tract of country known as Dartmoor is situated in South Devon, and, according to a report by Dr. Berger, in Moore's history of the county, contains nearly three hundred and fifty square miles of surface. Other authorities, however, estimate it to be considerably less in extent, the difference arising accordingly as the several commons lying near what is now considered as Dartmoor proper, have been included or not. These commons partake of its character to a very great degree, and undoubtedly at no distant time formed a part of it. There is a large extent of moorland lying to the eastward of Moretonhampstead and Lustleigh, bounded by the river Teign, which De la Beche, in his *Report on the Geology of Cornwall, Devon, and West Somerset*, considers to be both geologically and geographically a part of Dartmoor, and it was by including this and other similar tracts, that Dr. Berger arrived at the estimate he has given of its size. These portions of moorland have, however, been cut off by cultivation from the moor proper, and have not been included by the other authorities when making their estimates.

In the report of a Committee of the House of Commons, made in the early years of the nineteenth century, the size of the moor is given as one hundred and thirty thousand acres, or two hundred and three square miles, and this we may consider to be the extent of what is now generally known as Dartmoor.

The market towns and principal villages on its borders are Okehampton, Chagford, Moretonhampstead, Ashburton, Holne, South Brent, Ivybridge, Cornwood, Plympton, Shaugh, Meavy, Walkhampton, Tavistock, Lydford and Bridestowe. Its most southerly point is at the foot of the Western Beacon above Ivybridge, and the distance from this spot to its northern verge, immediately above the market town of Okehampton, is, as the crow flies, about twenty-three miles. Its average breadth is about ten or twelve miles, though at its widest part, from Black Down on the west to Ilsington Common on the east, it is over seventeen.

The elevation of Dartmoor is between one thousand three hundred and one thousand four hundred feet, while many of its hills attain an altitude of one thousand seven hundred or one thousand eight hnndred feet, and some over two thousand, the highest being on its borders.

Many of the hills are crowned with a rugged pile of granite rocks, known as a tor, which frequently assume grand and fantastic proportions. Numerous rivers take their rise in the bogs which are found in many of its more elevated parts, among which are the Dart (which gives name to the district), Teign, Taw, Ockment, Tavy, Walkham, Plym, Yealm, Erme, and the Avon, each having a number of tributaries. Its principal river, the Dart, is sometimes erroneously stated to have been so called from the swiftness of its current, which, however, is not more rapid than that of other streams on the moor. In all probability the the name is derived from the Celtic word *dwr*—water—a root found in the names of several rivers in countries peopled by Celtic tribes.

In some of the more desolate parts of Devon's lonely region the eye rests upon nothing but a vast stretch of heath, with here and there a tor, peeping over the gloomy looking ridges, a desert waste, from which even the faintest signs of civilization are absent. In other parts are deep valleys down which rush foaming torrents over rocky beds, the precipitous sides being clothed with furze and heather, with many a huge granite boulder half hidden in the wild and tangled growth, the numerous tors lifting high their rugged crests and standing like giant sentinels around.

King John disafforested the whole of the County of Devon, with the exception of Dartmoor and Exmoor, and though the former when it was afterwards bestowed upon Richard, Earl of Cornwall, by his brother, Henry III., ceased to be a forest in law, since none but a king can hold such unless by special warrant, it has nevertheless continued to be regarded as a forest down to our own day, and is generally so called. It is part of the Duchy of Cornwall, and is consequently always held by the male heir apparent to the throne, as duke, but in the event of their being none such, it reverts to the Crown for the time being. Perambulations have been made from time to time for the purpose of defining the limits of the forest, which lies in the centre of the moorland region, its boundaries being, in some parts, several miles from the cultivated country. The intervening tract, which presents similar characteristics to the forest, was formerly known as the Commons of Devonshire. It is made up of parts of a number of parishes surrounding the forest, many of which possess Venville rights, as certain privileges of pasturage and turbary are termed. The forest itself lies entirely within the parish of Lydford.

The return of a perambulation made in the year 1240 when Richard, Earl of Cornwall, was the lord of Dartmoor, sets forth the bounds of the forest, and of this there are several copies extant. A survey of the forest was also made in 1609, and the bounds as named in this, approach very closely to those generally recognised at the present time. These are defined by natural objects, such as a hill, a tor, or a river. The forest is divided into quarters, of which the north is the largest.

Ancient customs still survive on Dartmoor, though gradually giving place to modern usages. Yet it is still a home for many of our old superstitions and legendary tales, a place where much that found favour with our ancestors, and which, perhaps with questionable taste, is now voted out of fashion, still finds a refuge, and where freedom from all artificiality may be enjoyed. The artist may there find ample employment for his pencil, the disciple of Walton may revel to the full in the pursuit of his art. The geologist, the botanist, or the antiquary have there a rich field in which to indulge their various tastes, and the lover of nature can never tire of the delights afforded by a ramble through the secluded valleys, and over the breezy hills of wild and rugged Dartmoor.

But while the interior of the moor bears the palm for grandeur and sublimity, it is on its borders that one must look for the fairer and more beautiful scenes, where nature's softer features are exhibited in striking contrast to the sterner aspect of the moor.

Here are deep combes, having their sides partially cultivated, or clothed with thick coppices of oak, running far up into the wilds, in many of them more than one substantially built farmhouse of ancient date nestling in some sheltered nook, often in close proximity to a rugged tor; narrow gorges, through which the rivers leave their mountain birth-place, affording a glimpse of the barrenness beyond; steep hillsides rising from enclosures formed by roughly constructed granite walls, man's handiwork being of a ruder and more primitive style as the confines of the moor are approached; roads winding by the base of these frontier heights, often carried over the streams that rush impetuously down the valleys, by grey stone bridges, forming picturesque objects, which the artist delights to pourtray; quiet villages and hamlets on the very verge of the waste, the low towers of the little churches formed of granite from the rocky piles that rise so near to them; and somewhat further removed, the small market towns we have named, now brought more into communication with the larger centres of population, but which for centuries slept quietly in the shadow of the ancient hills.

No district in our country can boast of so great a number of rude stone remains as Dartmoor, every part of it furnishing examples of most of the pre-historic monuments known to the antiquary. And it is also rich in relics of mediæval times, and among these the stone cross is certainly not the least interesting. But of all the objects of antiquity few have, perhaps, come down to us in so mutilated a condition as this—the one we should expect would have had bestowed upon it the greatest care. Not only did the wayside and village cross suffer at a time when men's mistaken zeal caused them to commit acts of destruction in and around our churches, but in quite recent years they have received, in too many instances, but little consideration. In the one case the guiding influence was bigotry; in the other, ignorance or apathy. The latter, it is pleasing to know, are being removed; the former we can pity, without being so uncharitable as to blame. There is, in truth, no room for blame. The men who cast out the graven images from the churches, and overturned and shattered the sculptured stones by the wayside and on the village green, warred not against the cross, but against idolatry.

Apart from the interest attaching to the cross as a symbol of Christianity, it has other claims on our attention. No object in our island belonging to historic times is older. It existed before the earliest churches, for without doubt the latter came to the cross—the cross did not come to them. Where it was reared, people gathered for worship, and believers had before their eyes that which would cause them to remember the great work accomplished for mankind, as in days remote the stones set up in the sacred river reminded the Israelites of their deliverance from bondage. There is a tradition connected with the church and cross at North Lew, a parish to the north of Dartmoor, which tells us that the latter was anciently a preaching station of the monks of Tavistock. After a time a church was commenced to be built. First one aisle, then a second and a third, and so the structure was gradually completed.

But the cross, though no longer needed for its original purpose when each parish had its church, remained still an object of veneration, while within the sacred building its place was supplied by the great rood. And as it had been during long years the one point to which the little community were drawn for worship, so it came to be looked upon as the common centre of the village, and from it tidings were proclaimed in which the people were interested, and much took place around it that affected the common weal.

An object that could turn the thoughts to an event of such importance as the great sacrifice once offered for mankind, was peculiarly fitted for setting up in such places as the wayfarer might pass, for it became a guide to him in a double sense.

And thus by the track that led from town to town, and by the lonely paths over the bleak and barren hills, was the cross erected, that he who journeyed might feel certain of his way. Where a road diverged from, or was crossed by another, it was frequently placed* As the old tracks on Dartmoor were in many cases nothing more than a grassy path, and in places scarcely to be distinguished, such marks were of the greatest utility, and no doubt often safely guided the traveller when pursuing his way over the hills of the silent moor.

As a bond-mark, too, was the cross particularly suitable. The importance in early times of such being respected was very great, and an object reverenced as was the cross would become an efficient guard against encroachments. Many of the possessions of religious houses had their boundaries so defined, as is evidenced by records wherein these are named, not always by crosses set up for the purpose perhaps, but by adapting those already existing. That some of the crosses in the Dartmoor country also marked the limits of a sanctuary is not improbable.

The cross was also erected at the place of burial. In very remote times we know it was the custom to raise a stone pillar as a monument over the dead, and in the early days of Christianity the cross took its place. The ancient observance was not given up, the form of the monument was simply changed, and the old menhir and the inscribed stone gave way to the symbol of the new faith. It is indeed most likely that the very earliest crosses were those connected with the rites of sepulture. The sacred emblem was at first merely inscribed upon the rude pillar, until at length men began to give the latter the shape of the former, and so the cross was gradually substituted for the upright stone.

The crosses which are to be found on Dartmoor, like most of the Devonshire examples, are of simple form, and cannot boast of the beauty which belongs to some of those existing to the westward of the Tamar. A few only possess any

---

*They are often seen in such situations, and the former existence of others is revealed by the names of many places upon our highways and in our lanes. It is not, however, suggested that this is always the case when the word "Cross" is affixed to a name; sometimes it means nothing more than a cross-road.

ornamentation, and that in a very slight degree; and, with one or two exceptions, no inscriptions are to be seen on them.

Their surroundings, however, invest them with a charm peculiarly their own ; for we cannot behold these old lichen-stained and weather-beaten memorials of the past, standing in close proximity to the remains of the rude habitations of the Celts, without contrasting in our minds the dark times when those huts were peopled, with the clear daylight which beamed forth when the cross was planted, and with the blessings which Christianity has spread over the land.

Among the grey tors they stand in solitude—the far-stretching heath on every side—with no sound to break the stillness that reigns around but that of the rushing of the streams from the rugged hill-sides. As we gaze upon them, we can let our thoughts stray back to the time when they were first reared, and in fancy may see the wondrous events which have since taken place on the stage of this world's vast theatre. Nor will it fail to strike us how little have all these events affected what we can see around us. The granite tors still lift their lofty heads to the sky, the heather and gorse still bloom on the moor, the stream yet pursues its way over its rocky bed, and all is here unchanged. While events which have shaken the outside world, and have decided the fate of nations, have been occurring, these hills and valleys, huge rocks and winding streams, have remained as in the days of old, and these venerable stone crosses have been lost in the solitariness of the moorlands.

At early morn when all is fresh and bright, when the dew-drops sparkle on the heather,

"And drowned in yonder living blue,
The lark becomes a sightless song,"

the impressionable mind will experience a pleasurable emotion at beholding here, far from the haunts of man, the emblem of the Christian faith. At the hour of sunset, when the shades of evening are beginning to settle over the wilds, and we hear that moaning sound so peculiar to the Dartmoor rivers as the twilight approaches, a calm feeling steals over us, which is heightened when, perchance, we find ourselves beside an old granite cross, alone on the heath ; and when night spreads her dark robe over mountain and plain, and the sole light is that which is lent by the pale stars, that form will forcibly remind us of the power which the religion of the cross has exercised over the darkness of our land, and which it has so happily dispelled.

The hands that fashioned these time-worn relics have long since mouldered in the tomb; and they themselves are ofttimes overturned and shattered, deeply impressing us as we contemplate their ruin, with the certainty that all the works of man will fall and crumble away before the touch of Time.

And in many of the rural settlements around the great uplands, and on the roads that lead to them, we shall also meet with the objects which it is now our purpose to examine. Some of these will, of course, differ in character from those that exist upon the moor itself; for here the market-cross and the churchyard-cross will claim a share of our attention, while on the waste they were set up either to mark a boundary, or as guides to the wayfarer. And the difference is not only in their character, for although the crosses of the moorland borders display little elaboration in their fashioning, yet there are few of quite so rude a type as the examples seen on the moor itself. We shall not be disappointed, however, in our examination of them, though we do find them lack ornamentation, for there is much in them and their associations to interest and attract, while the scenery amid which we shall roam as we visit in turn these venerable memorials, will not fail to call forth our admiration, and constitute an additional delight.

In our ramble we shall seldom stray far from the old moor, and it will not need that we look towards its hills to tell us of its proximity, for nearly every step we take will remind us of this. The old-fashioned farm-house with its wide porch and parvise room, and mullioned windows, and the lowly thatched cottage, alike of granite; and boulders partly covered with moss, and half-hidden by ferns, by the sides of many of the narrow lanes, will all plainly reveal that we are near the land of tors, and will cause us to realise when we sometimes wander by enclosed fields, and by the dwellings of men, that we are yet in the Dartmoor country.

CHAPTER II.

The Boundary Crosses of Brent Moor.

Brent Hill—Brent Fair—Church of St. Patrick—Christopher Jellinger—Brent Market Cross—Hobajon's Cross—Old Map of Dartmoor—Butterdon Stone Row—Three Barrows—Western Whitaburrow—Petre's Cross—Sir William Petre—Buckland Ford—The Abbots' Way—Clapper Bridge—Huntingdon Cross—The Valley of the Avon.

On the left bank of the Avon, a stream that has its source in a solitary part of the south quarter of the forest, as the central portion of the great moor is termed, is situated the small market town of South Brent, and it is here that we shall commence our ramble. It is distant some mile and a half from the confines of the moor, to which several roads lead. Immediately to the north of it rises a lofty eminence known as Brent Hill, and on the west it is overlooked by the Eastern Beacon on Ugborough Moor.

The chief attraction in the immediate vicinity of the town is the first-named height, whence is commanded a most extensive view, the beauty of which amply compensates the visitor for the toil of the ascent. The greater part of the South Hams of Devon lies, as it were, at the feet of the beholder, while in the other direction is a grand sweep of moor, with the ridge of Hameldon rising huge and bold against the northern sky.

On the summit of Brent Hill are the scanty ruins of a small building, locally reported to have been a chapel. It is also stated to be the remains of a windmill, erected towards the end of the eighteenth century by Dr. Tripe, of Ashburton. What truth there is in this I know not, but if any, it would seem more probable that he converted some ancient building to his purpose. Many years ago I learnt from one who remembered when much more of the ruin than now exists was standing, that the walls were pierced with loop holes, and he had always heard that it was used as a "look-out house."

Whether this was so, and it had ever served the purpose of a place of shelter to the watchers of the beacon fire, I am unable to offer an opinion, but that such blazed upon this prominent height, there seems little reason to doubt.*

Less than half a mile to the northward of Brent Hill, and by the side of the road that leads from Lutton Green to Gigley Bridge, is a small marshy spot known as Bloody Pool, though it is only in very wet seasons that much water can be seen there. What were supposed to be weapons of bronze, but which are in reality the heads of ancient fishing spears, were found there many years since, and may be seen in the Albert Memorial Museum at Exeter.

The manor and church of Brent belonged from a very early period to the Abbey of Buckfast; after the Dissolution, the former was bestowed upon Sir William Petre, and in 1806 a great portion of it was sold. There are two fairs yearly, and Risdon tells us this was so in his time, but more anciently it seems to have been held once a year only, at Michaelmas, and lasted for three days. According to Risdon, one fair was on May-day, and the other on St. Michael's-day, but in 1778, more than a century and a half after our topographer wrote his *Survey of Devon*, the days on which they still continue to be held were fixed. The fairs commence at noon on the Monday before the last Tuesday in the months of April and September, and continue till the Wednesday night; but the Tuesday is now the day of the actual fair. The old custom of holding it "*under the glove*" is not departed from, the glove being raised upon a pole when the fair commences, and kept there during its continuance. This still prevails in many towns and villages, and is an ancient form of charter; a glove sent to the inhabitants was a token that the rights prayed for were granted.

---

* If a signalling station so near to the Eastern Beacon on Ugborough Moor should seem to have been unnecessary, it may be well to explain that it is doubtful whether that ever was a beacon hill. The name appears to be a corruption of Pigedon, by which appellation it was anciently known, according to an old map of Dartmoor, now in the Albert Memorial Museum at Exeter. On the same map, the moorgate at the foot of the hill (now called Peek Gate) is marked as Picke Yeat, and old people in the neighbourhood used to speak of the height as Picken Hill. Brent Hill would also seem to be the more suitable of the two for the purpose of signalling.

The parish church dedicated to St. Patrick is situated at one end of the little town, on a knoll, at the foot of which flows the Avon. The tower is of earlier date than the church, and is of late Norman character, with some Early English additions. The occurrence of arches in the bottom stage, point to its having been the central tower of a Norman church, and the building now used as a vestry appears to have formed one of the transepts of this early structure. Although in four stages the tower is not of great height.

The font is of red sandstone, and is most beautifully carved, being of the late conventional Norman type.

In the fifteenth century a vicar of the parish was murdered in the church, and when it was restored about the year 1870 under the direction of Mr. James Hine, of Plymouth, some highly finished portions of a recumbent effigy and tomb were discovered, which Mr. Hine conjectured to belong to the tomb of this vicar. In 1436 Bishop Lacy reconciled the church, after its profanation by the murder.

Christopher Jellinger, one of the ministers ejected from the Church of England by the Act of Uniformity, in 1662, was sometime vicar of this parish. He was born near Worms, and studied at Basil and Leyden. After the Restoration the Marquis of Winchester offered to prefer him if he would conform, but true to his principles, he refused. He died at Kingsbridge, at the ripe age of 83 years, continuing to preach when he was very old.

The ringers of Brent observe some quaint customs at their annual meeting and supper, duly electing for the year "a lord chief" and a "crier." Their signatures are then entered in the "ringers' book," which dates back to 1789.

A few years ago Brent had its cross; now ignorance has done its work, and it no longer exists. Within living recollection it stood against the wall of the old market house, which was demolished many years ago. The cross was then removed to a court behind the Anchor Hotel, where it lay neglected until a very few years since, when a builder broke it up and carted it off to a building he was erecting in the parish of Diptford. It is lamentable that such things should be. The cross was the only antiquity Brent possessed, and that has been suffered to be destroyed. The shaft and arms were octagonal in shape, and the former tapered slightly. Its height was five and a half feet, and across the arms it measured two feet seven inches.

But though there is no cross now in Brent itself, the moor belonging to the parish can furnish us with an example, and, for the purpose of examining this, and others on the boundary line of the forest, we shall leave the little town, and direct our steps to Three Barrows, a lofty hill rising high above the left bank of the Erme. Our way will first take us by the foot of Splatton Hill to Lydia or Leedy Bridge, a single arch spanning the Avon. Immediately above it is a fine waterfall, while below a stately row of beeches throw their branches partly over the stream, along the bank of which is a path leading by the vicarage lawn to the church. Passing up the hill, we reach the hamlet of Aish, at the higher end of which we turn into a lane on the left, and, still ascending, at length enter upon the common known as Aish Ridge.

From this elevated down Three Barrows can be plainly seen, and for some considerable distance we shall have the advantage of a moorland track which runs towards it. This path will bring us to Brent Moor at Coryndon Ball Gate, soon after which we shall commence the ascent of the hill, where, on the slope near the summit, we shall find the shattered remains of one of the objects it is now our purpose to examine, lying amid the granite with which the ground is strewed.

Three Barrows, which is about three and a half miles from Brent and some two miles to the northward of Harford Church, is crowned with three large cairns, whence its name, and during an exploration of one of them by Mr. Spence Bate, recorded in the fifth volume (1872) of the *Transactions of the Devonshire Association*, part of a cross, consisting of one of the arms and the top of the shaft, was found near at hand. This he, with great probability, supposed to be a portion of one which he states was set up by a jury of survey, empanelled to settle some bounds in this part of the moor about a century and a half before.

He also considered that in it he saw all that remained of a cross which is mentioned on an old map of Dartmoor as Hobajon's Cross, and which is there represented as standing on two steps, and is situated nearly in the middle of a row of upright stones. This row extends from Butterdon Hill, near the Western Beacon above Ivybridge, to within a short distance of Sharp Tor, which overlooks the enclosure known as Piles Newtake. At the former place it is seen leading directly from a circle thirty-five feet in diameter, of which the stones, with the exception of two (and those partially so) are fallen. This encloses a small cairn about twenty feet in diameter, much dilapidated.

It has been supposed that the old map in question dates back as far as 1240, in which year a perambulation of the forest was made, or even earlier; but, as Mr. J. Brooking Rowe points out in his *Cistercian Houses of Devon*,* this cannot be the case, because on it there is a representation of the Abbey Church of Buckland, which abbey was not founded until 1278. He considers it to be of two centuries later date. Further on, I shall bring forward some evidence which I think will show that this view is the more correct one; but without going into this question now, it certainly appears from the map that a cross was standing in the stone-row at the time it was drawn, but I am not so sure that it was ever fixed on steps as it is there represented. Another cross, which we shall notice hereafter, is shown on the map as standing on steps in the same manner, although nothing of the sort is to be seen near it now, so that it is possible that this was no more than a conventional mode of the draughtsman to indicate the existence of these crosses, and it was not, perhaps, intended, or considered necessary, to convey a perfectly correct idea of their form.

Mr. Bate accounts for the cross being erected in the stone-row on the hypothesis that those who reared it, finding the dark clouds of superstition clinging to the heathen relic, were anxious to plant the symbol of Christianity amid the rude erections of the Pagans. This, indeed, may have been the case, but I am inclined to think it quite as probable that the cross was set up simply as a boundary mark. When the object for which the stone-row was primarily erected was forgotten, it was naturally looked upon as a boundary, and still continues to serve as such, constituting, as far as it extends, the line which divides Ugborough and Harford

---

* Trans. Devon Assoc., Vol. vii., p. 345.

Moors. As fresh perambulations of the bounds were made, in all likelihood new marks were added, and Hobajon's Cross we may not unreasonably consider to be one of these.

The mutilated cross which is at present to be seen, consists, as stated, of the top of the shaft and one of the arms only. The arm is ten inches in length, the shaft measuring sixteen inches from its upper surface, and being about fourteen inches in width. As the sides of it, however, are not quite parallel, the width is not the same throughout, but is rather greater at the top. It must have been a massive cross when in its complete state, with a breadth across the arms of about two feet eight inches; its height, of course, it is impossible to determine. The fracture runs across obliquely from under the remaining arm. One side of the shaft is ten inches in thickness, the other only seven inches. It is now lying on the slope of the hill toward the river Erme, not far from the north-western cairn.

From the absence of any other cross near the spot, I think we may safely conclude that this is the one that the jury, of whom Mr. Bate speaks, erected on one of the cairns on this hill; and that it is also the old Hobajon's Cross is nearly certain, for, although the existence of this mutilated head is not generally known, the name still lingers here—a small heap of stones at no great distance from the top of the hill being called by the moormen Hobajon's Cross.

This point forms the starting place when the bounds of a portion of the moor in this locality, over which the lord of the manor of Ermington exercises certain rights, are perambulated—the first record of such perambulation being in the year 1603.

If the supposition be correct, as no doubt it is, that we now see on Three Barrows a portion of this ancient cross, we know that it must have been brought from the stone-row, as we have no reason to consider the map wrong in representing it as standing there, but other hands, I think, than those of the jury of survey did this. From the fact of the manor boundary mark bearing the name of Hobajon's Cross, it would seem likely that at one time it was erected there, in which case we should perhaps be inclined to consider that those who were engaged in marking out those bounds, were concerned in the removal of the cross; but I am of opinion that they were not those who took it from its original position, although it is not impossible that they may have used it as a mark for their boundary,

In the account of Buckfast Abbey in Dr. Oliver's *Monasticon* there is an inquisition on the boundary of Brent Moor, dated 1557,* at which time certain rights and privileges pertaining to it were held by Sir William Petre in virtue of his possession of the manor of South Brent. This boundary line was marked by four crosses at certain points; one on the centre cairn at Three Barrows, one on the cairn known as Western Whitaburrow, a third at Buckland Ford, and a fourth at the confluence of the Avon, or Aune, with the Western Wellabrook, and they each had the words " Bunda de Brentmore," engraven on their faces. I am inclined to believe that it was for the purpose of serving as a mark to these bounds that Hobajon's Cross was taken from the row of stones, and if it ever stood on the little cairn marking the boundary of the lands over which the manorial rights of Ermington extend, it was taken there from Three Barrows, in which case the jury of survey, to whom Mr. Bate has alluded, must have found it there, and set it up once more upon the great cairn on the hill. There is no trace of any inscription to be seen on the portion which now remains of this interesting relic, and how it became so mutilated it is impossible to say.

I have carefully examined the stone-row on several occasions, but could never find any traces of the steps as shown on the map, and, as before observed, it is doubtful whether they ever existed.

On a stone at the extreme end of a row† nearest Sharp Tor, and which is much larger than most of the others which compose it, is a small incised cross measuring seven inches in height and five and a half inches across. This stone is evidently an addition to the row, but is distinguishable, at a glance, from a modern boundary post. It stands about three and a half feet above the ground, and appears to mark some important point, as it is placed in the middle of a small, rough

---

* Monasticon Dioecesis Exoniensis, p. 378.

† From its commencement at the circle on Butterdon Hill, to its termination at this stone, the row is one thousand seven hundred and ninety-one yards in length. The distance of the centre cairn on Three Barrows from the stone is two thousand three hundred and twenty-five yards.

circular pavement, about six feet nine inches in diameter. May we not allow that there is a probability that this inscribed stone marks the spot where, in years long since flown, the old cross was standing, and that it was set up, after the removal of the latter, as a memorial of it by those who were interested in preserving these particular bounds? I do not forget that the map represents Hobajon's Cross as being in the centre of the stone-row, and this stone as I have said, is at its end; but the row is continued from this point by modern boundary stones, and in all probability was so continued by older bond-marks at the time the map was drawn, so that if the cross really stood on the spot in question, in placing it in the middle of the row, the map would be substantially correct.

There is one consideration we must not overlook, which is, that it would not have been a very difficult task to remove the cross from Three Barrows, and to have re-erected it in the row, instead of setting up another stone there in its place. But it is not unlikely that it was found to be broken, though perhaps not in such a mutilated state as we see it now, and was no longer in a condition to be placed in its old position.

The view from the commanding height of Three Barrows, or as old records have it, Threberis, is one of great variety and beauty. A large portion of the country lying between the southern frontier of Dartmoor and the Channel is spread out before us, and most of the prominent headlands on the South Devonshire coast are plainly visible. On the other side we look into the moor. Away to the northward is seen the boggy land in the neighbourhood of Erme Head, with the distant tors peeping over the dark brown ridges. Westward the river flows at a great distance below the wind-swept height on which we stand, and Piles Wood is discernible far down the steep, stretching along the bank of the stream.

Before leaving Three Barrows we must not omit to observe the fine reave, or boundary bank, which runs up from the East Glaze to the centre cairn, and pursues its course down the slope of the hill towards a little stream that falls into the Erme.

Proceeding in a northerly direction we shall make our way to Western Whitaburrow, one of the bounds of the forest; and in so doing shall follow the line of posts that mark the boundary of Brent Moor, which boundary appears to be indicated on the old map by a line on which are placed what seems to be meant for three stones.

The cairn which bears the name of Western Whitaburrow is sixty-three yards in circumference, and according to the inquisition alluded to, the second cross marked with the words "Bunda de Brentmore" was placed here. Until about the year 1847 it was to be seen erect on the centre of the cairn; but it was then partially destroyed by some workmen in the employ of a company which was formed for the purpose of extracting naphtha from the peat that here abounds, but the undertaking was not a success. The works were close to Shipley Bridge, and the peat was taken thither from this spot on tram-waggons; the old tram-road is now in a very ruinous condition, but still serves as a bridle-path.

There being no place of shelter near, the labourers erected a house on the cairn with the stones of which it was composed, and, requiring a large stone as a support for the chimney-breast, they knocked off the arms of the cross and used the shaft for that purpose. I learnt this over thirty years ago from one of the men who had been employed on the works at the time, and gleaned further facts concerning the cross from others, who had then long known the moor. It may here be well to correct a statement that appeared in a guide-book, published about three years since, to the effect that the cross was discovered by the Ordnance surveyors at a *"factory building near Didworthy."* There is no foundation whatever for it. The house at the cairn has been taken down for many years; the walls, to the height of about three or four feet, being all that is now to be seen of it, but the shaft of the cross has, fortunately, not been lost. It is now set up on the cairn, and has had the broad arrow cut on it by the Ordnance surveyors. It measures four feet in height, and about fifteen inches in width. At the end which is now uppermost there is a tenon, and I therefore take this to be the bottom of the shaft, which was so fashioned in order that it might fit into a socket. The name of it, too, is still unforgotten, for the spot is seldom called by its older appellaton of Whitaburrow,* but is generally known as Petre's Cross.

Sir William Petre, of whom Prince in his *Worthies of Devon* gives us an account, and who was, as already stated, the possessor of certain rights over Brent Moor was born at Tor Newton, in the parish of Tor Brian. He was Secretary of State in four reigns, those of Henry VIII., Edward VI., Mary, and Elizabeth; and, it is said of him that in this office he was "smooth, reserved, resolved, and yet obliging." He amassed great wealth derived from the monastic possessions which were granted to him. He died in 1571, and was buried at Ingatestone in Essex.

Our search for the third cross will take us to Buckland Ford—so we shall make our way down the hill in a north-easterly direction, and passing a bound-stone, shall soon reach the foot of a steep narrow gully, close to which we shall observe an old path, which we shall descend for a short distance to a point where it crosses a small stream which falls into the Avon just below. This is Buckland Ford, but we shall look in vain for the cross. This ford is shown on some maps as being on the Avon. This is wrong; it is the crossing-place over a tributary of that river, as above described. It doubtless was so called in consequence of being on the monks' path leading to Buckland. I have carefully searched around the spot, yet have never been able to find it, nor can I learn that any one has ever seen it. Some mining operations appear to have been carried on near the bank of the Avon, and it is possible that the cross may have been destroyed by those who were concerned in them.

The old track which crosses the stream at this ford is called the Abbots' Way, and can be traced from Dean Moor for several miles, passing the source of the Erme, and the head waters of the Plym. It formed a direct means of com-

---

*So spelt with the addition of an *e* in the survey of the forest of 1609; in the perambulation of 1240, the name is spelled Whyteburghe. It is Eastern Whitaburrow, however which is mentioned in these perambulations, and not Western Whitaburrow. The cairn known as Eastern Whitaburrow is ninety yards in circumference, and twelve yards in height. The name is pronounced with the *i* long, as though spelled White-a-burrow,

munication between the abbeys of Buckland and Tavistock on one side of the moor, and Buckfast on the other. The name by which I have always heard it called by the moor-men is Jobbler's or Jobber's Path, which it doubtless obtained from being used by the yarn-jobbers in former days. The monks of Buckfast were extensive traders in wool, and this commodity and yarn spun from it, no donbt often formed the loads which were carried on the backs of horses on this old road. It appears more than probable that it passed near where Princetown now stands, for I find that Mr. Burt in his preface to Carrington's *Dartmoor*, published in 1826, states that traces of a trackway called Jobbers' Cross were visible across bogs near the prison.

Although we shall be unsuccessful in finding the cross at Buckland Ford, we shall be well repaid for having visited the spot, for the surroundings combine to form a most pleasing picture of a moorland valley, secluded and quiet, and closed in by hills on every hand. Behind us stretches the heathery slope known as Bush Meads, anciently Bishop's Meads; to our left (in summer time covered thickly with ferns) a hill rises precipitously from the Avon, which here bends round in a fine sweep. On our right hand the bottom of the valley is shut in by Dean Moor, and immediately in front of us, on the opposite side of the river, is Huntingdon Warren, a find bold hill of good hard ground, free from heather, but covered in places with scattered granite. Several enclosures, the rude erection of the Danmonii, are in sight, and tell us that this quiet valley was once thickly peopled by the ancient inhabitants of the moor.

Not far from where we stand the Avon is spanned by a rude bridge of two openings, formed of slabs laid on a centre pier, consisting partly of the natural rock.* Further up the

---

*Bridges formed of huge flat stones laid upon rudely wrought abutments and piers, are termed clappers, and are almost peculiar to the Dartmoor country. This bridge, although constructed in a precisely similar manner to those which are undoubtedly of some age, is distinguishable from them at a glance. Here the edges of the granite are not rounded as they are in the older examples. The two stones which form the roadway and which once were evidently one, show the marks of wedges used in spliting them. I have been told that it was built by the first owner of the warren, which was formed early in the nineteenth century. The bridge however, presents a very picturesque appearance.

stream is a craggy hollow, though we can see little of it, from which the river issues. It there falls in a series of small cascades and widely spreading rivulets over a number of rocky ledges, placed at the head of the solitary glen.

From Buckland Ford we shall follow the Abbots' Way to the Avon, and tracing the river downward shall cross it at another ford, at a spot known to the moormen as Lower Huntingdon Corner, immediately above the confluence of the stream with the Western Wellabrook. It is here the inquisition says, the fourth cross was set up, and we shall be gratified at observing it standing erect a few yards from the bank of the river. It is now known as Huntingdon Cross, and is situated at the corner of the warren. It is immediately within the forest bounds, and close to the spot where the parish of Lydford (in which the whole of the forest lies) joins the parishes of Dean and Brent.

Although the crosses at Buckland Ford and Lower Huntingdon Corner were claimed in 1557 as marking the boundary of Brent Moor, it is not at all probable that such was their original purpose. That, there is little doubt, was to mark the Abbots' Way, and they were adapted later as boundary stones But it is, nevertheless, certain that Brent Moor never extended to Buckland Ford. The Perambulation of 1240 and the Survey of 1609 both show that the forest boundary line runs from the confluence of the Wellabrook and the Avon to Eastern Whitaburrow, and not directly to Western Whitaburrow, so that Buckland Ford would lie some way within the forest. The placing of the Brent boundary at the latter spot was simply an encroachment on the duchy property, of which there are a number of similar instances in other paats of the moor.

The name Huntingdon is not improbably derived from *aun*, water (in this particular instance the name of the river which here flows by) and *dun*, a hill, *i,e.*, the water hill, which certainly commends itself as a very suitable apellation, for the latter is bounded on two sides by the Avon or Aune, and on a third by the Wellabrook.

Huntingdon Cross is romantically situated in a kind of hollow, the rising ground surrounding it being covered with patches of heather, with here and there a grey boulder of granite. All around is silent, save for the low murmuring of the waters as they run over their pebbly bed. The only signs of life are the furry inhabitants of the warren, and, perchance, a herd of Dartmoor ponies, wild as the country over which they roam, and a few sheep or cattle grazing on the slopes. The cross is surrounded by rushes, and a delapidated wall—the warren enclosure—runs near it. It stands a little out of the perpendicular, and is close upon four and a half feet in height. Across the arms it measures one foot ten inches. There is no trace whatever of any inscription to be seen upon it

Evidences of the occupancy of man, and of the works of his hand, are plainly visible in this spot. The Abbots' Way is here distinctly seen ascending the left bank of the river as it makes for the enclosed country above Dean Burn. Along the bank of the Wellabrook old mining operations have left their traces; and on the slope of the hill to the east is a large circular enclosure, two hundred and eighty yards in circumference, and between it and the Avon are nine hut circles. Further down the river these hut settlements are numerous, especially on the left bank.

With our examination of Huntingdon Cross we shall conclude the survey of the four which formerly served to mark the bounds of what was claimed as Brent Moor, and shall make our way down the valley of the Avon to Shipley Bridge, a distance of about three miles. Here, passing through the moor gate, we enter upon a lane which will conduct us to the hamlet of Aish, whence descending once more to Lydia Bridge, we shall return to South Brent.

CHAPTER III.

By the Southern Border Heights.

Ugborough Moor—Bagga's Bush—Old Guide-post—Sandowl Cross—Hookmoor Cross—Ugborough Church—Bishop Prideaux—Owley—Spurrell's Cross—Harford—Broomhill to Ivybridge.

The line of stone posts which we noticed in our progress from Three Barrows to Western Whitaburrow serves to mark the boundary between the moors of Brent and Ugborough. The latter common extends from the forest to the foot of the Eastern Beacon, near Wrangaton, thrusting its southern extremity into the cultivated country.

Not far from the foot of this is situated the village of Ugborough, and thither we shall now proceed, afterwards entering again upon the commons, and crossing them to the parish of Harford.

We shall leave Brent by the old Plymouth coach-road, and on crossing Brent Bridge shall find that it takes a course to the right of the present highway. About a quarter of a mile from the bridge is a spot called Bagga's Bush, near which is a stone worthy of a passing notice. It is an old guide-post, standing close by the roadside, small in size and barely thirty inches in height. On its face is the letter **M** denoting the direction of Modbury, the road, or lane, leading to that place, diverging a short distance further on. Its eastern and western sides bear respectively the letters **E** and **P**, standing for Exeter and Plymouth. The letters are cut in relief, two of them being much worn.

Following the Modbury lane we shall soon reach a bridge over the Glaze, a stream serving as a boundary between the parishes of Brent and Ugborough, just beyond which, near a wayside inn called the Carew Arms, we cross the modern road to Plymouth. The lane ascends the hill, and will lead us direct to the spot where we shall find the object that will next claim our attention.

This is a stone set up in the centre of a small open space, whence several roads diverge, named Sandowl Cross, but at

one time more generally known as Sign o' the Owl. It is
related that a hostelry once stood upon the spot, called *The
Owl*, whence the latter name. Whether there is any truth in
this I am unable to say, but I should be inclined to think not,
as the correct name seems to be Sandowl. The stone does
not appear to have ever been fashioned into the shape of a
cross; it is somewhat unsuitable for the shaft of such, nor
are there any traces of fracture, as would be the case had it
ever possessed a head and arms. But there is nothing in the
fact of the place bearing the name which it does, to cause us
to suppose that a cross must necessarily have once stood there,
for as already has been observed, cross-roads are sufficient to
confer such a title. The height of the stone above the ground
is about thirty-two inches, and it is about four feet in girth.
Its four sides nearly face the cardinal points, and on each,
near the top, is a letter, cut in relief. On the northern face
(or strictly speaking N.E. by N.) is the letter **B** which stands
for Brent, and points out the road by which we have approached the stone from that place. On another face is the
letter **T** indicating the direction of Totnes; on a third face the
letter **K** standing for Kingsbridge; and on a fourth the
letter **M**, one of the side strokes of which is somewhat worn,
meaning Modbury. The stone is very interesting as an old
guide-post, and the letters are similar in character to those
found upon other stones in quite a different part of the moorland borders.

There is a very good view of a portion of the south-eastern
frontier of Dartmoor from Sandowl Cross. The Eastern
Beacon looks quite near, but its appearance is not so fine as
when viewed from Brent. To the left of it is the Western
Beacon above Ivybridge, and to the right several prominent
heights on Brent Moor, with Brent Hill rising in the form
of a bold, conical peak.

The road to Modbury which passes through the village of
Ugborough, branches off on the right hand, a short distance
to the westward of Sandowl Cross, and it is this which we
shall now pursue. Very soon the road is crossed by another,
and immediately around the corner of the hedge on our right,
an object will be observed which will arouse our interest.
This is a small granite cross, somewhat rudely fashioned, and
a little weathered, though otherwise in a complete state. It

is leaning toward the hedge, but only slightly; its southern face fronts the road. It is known by the name of Hookmoor Cross, and served the same purpose as the stone we have just been examining, for on it are four letters cut in relief in a precisely similar manner. These letters are M B T and P standing respectively for Modbury, Brent, Totnes, and Plymouth. The first is placed between the arms on the southern face; the second occupies a like position on the northern face, now hidden, as it fronts the hedge; the third is cut on the end of the eastern arm, and the last on the end of the western one. The cross is two and a half feet in height, and measures fifteen inches across the arms, which are about seven or eight inches deep, and project about four inches from the shaft. This is the height also that the head, which is tapering, rises above them. Below the arms the shaft is only worked for a few inches, the bottom part of the stone from which the cross is formed being left in its original condition. Had the letters been incised we might have imagined that they were placed on the cross at a period subsequent to its first erection, but cut as they are in relief, it is evident that this was done at the time it was made, and it therefore becomes certain that the primary object of those who set it up was to point the way to the traveller, the emblem of his faith at the same time reminding him of the path he must pursue if he would safely accomplish that longer journey which ends only at the grave.

Pursuing the southern road for a short distance we shall come in sight of the village of Ugborough, and as we descend the hill leading to it we shall be struck with the very imposing appearance of its church, the noble sixteenth century tower rising to a height of nearly one hundred feet. The sacred edifice occupies a commanding position, upon rising ground on the southern side of a large open space, round which the houses of the village cluster, and is approached by a broad, semi-circular flight of granite steps.

We have seen that the tower at Brent is much older than the church; the reverse is the case at Ugborough, for here the church is of some two hundred years earlier date than the tower. Few country parishes in Devon can boast of one so large, and the ecclesiastical antiquary will find much in it of interest. There are a great number of finely carved bosses in the roof of the north aisle, three of them towards the western end being very remarkable. One represents a smith at work; another a sow suckling a litter of eight; and the third the head of a Turk. In the north transept, which was restored in 1862, is a stained window, with figures of the four evangelists, and in the east wall of the same is a brass, having engraved upon it the effigy of a female. It was discovered in the year just mentioned, close at hand, along with another, which was unfortunately destroyed. A portion only of the screen remains, but it is very beautifully carved.

A little over three hundred years ago Ugborough Church was the scene of a competition between two candidates for the post of parish clerk. In order to decide between them, an arrangement was made that they should "tune the psalm," and this was accordingly carried out. The one who was defeated was John Prideaux, of Stowford, in the adjoining parish of Harford, and he felt the disappointment very keenly. But it was the means of introducing him to higher things. Not long after he left Ugborough and made his way to Oxford. Working first in the kitchen of Exeter College, he devoted all his spare time to study, and was at length admitted to its literary privileges. In three years he took the degree of Bachelor of Arts, and was afterwards raised by Charles I. to a bishopric. "If I could have been parish clerk of Ugborough," he used to say, "I had never been Bishop of Worcester."

In the parish of Ugborough was born in 1620, Sir John Kempthorn, an eminent naval commander, who in engagements with the Turks and Dutch proved himself a brave officer.

A relic of pre-historic times was found in 1889, on Woodland Farm. This was a stone adze, $3\frac{7}{8}$ inches in length, $2\frac{5}{16}$ inches in breadth, the hole in it measuring 1 inch by $\frac{7}{8}$ of an inch. In the portion of this parish that lies upon Dartmoor are not a few interesting memorials of the people who at an early period made the wild hills their home.

Bidding Ugborough and its church adieu, we shall make our way to Owley Gate, which opens on to Ugborough Moor, below the Eastern Beacon, and for this purpose shall retrace our steps to Sandowl Cross, and thence proceed to Wrangaton Station. Crossing the line and entering the lane leading to the moor, a walk of about a mile and a half will bring us to the gate. Here we shall observe a rough track, pursuing which for a short distance, and crossing the head of a little brook, we shall find it has become a smooth green path of considerable width. By following this grassy road, which runs nearly due east and west, and which we shall be well able to do, even after it loses its present character and is covered with heather, for it is marked throughout the whole of its course by small heaps of stones placed at short distances apart, we shall reach the moor gate at Harford. This path forms the most direct route to that place from Owley or from Brent.

We shall find the object of which we are in quest about a mile from the gate by which we have entered on the moor. It is the top of the shaft, and one of the arms of a very curious old cross, and it is much to be lamented that it has been so mutilated. It is known as Spurrell's Cross (though the moormen sometimes call it Purl's) and is situated by the side of the path we have been following, close to the point where it is intersected by an old road, which though now exhibiting the marks of wheels and showing us that it is sometimes used as a way for bringing in peat, is very probably an ancient track, and can be traced a considerable distance. It passes between Sharp Tor and Three Barrows, and goes direct to Left Lake Ford, and from thence to one of the boundary stones of Ugborough and Harford Moors. From this point it becomes a narrow path, but can be followed as far as Hook Lake, a stream that runs down the hollow called Stony Bottom and falls into the Erme. Erme Pound is at no great distance from that hollow, and a little to the north of it the Abbots' Way crosses Red Lake. South of the cross this track may be traced to the enclosed lands below the Eastern Beacon.

The shaft of Spurrell's Cross is missing, and the mutilated head is simply fixed up on a few loose stones. There is little doubt, however, that, being found at the intersection of paths, it is now on its original site, or within a short distance of it.

But besides marking the track from Owley and the one which crosses it, it also served to indicate the direction of another. This latter ran from Buckfast to Plympton, and joins the Owley path not far from where the cross is seen. I have traced it for several miles along the verge of the moor. It crossed the Erme at Harford and went through Cornwood, and thence to Plympton by way of Sparkwell.

Although what remains of Spurrell's Cross is but a fragment, it is sufficient to show that it possessed a certain amount of roughly executed ornamentation. It appears to have been cylindrical in shape, and across the upper and under surfaces of the arm there are projections about an inch and a half high, and about two and a half inches wide. The same are also to be observed on each side of the top of the shaft, the only part of this which is now remaining. These must have given the cross a very interesting appearance, when in its complete state. There is no other example of a Dartmoor cross in which this rude kind of ornamentation occurs, nor is there anything of the sort to be observed on those which are pourtrayed in Blight's *Ancient Crosses and Antiquities of Cornwall*.

The portion that is left to us of this interesting relic measures from the top of the shaft to the fracture, which is immediately below the arms, one foot eleven inches. One arm is completely gone, and the end of the other is also broken. From the present extremity of this arm to the further side of the shaft from where the other has been broken off, the measurement is one foot five inches. From the upper surface of the arm to the top of the shaft it is nine and a half inches, and the diameter of the arm is about one foot.

It presents a very weather-beaten appearance, and, though ornamented in the manner described, is rougher on its surface than most of the crosses that are found on the moor. This, however, may have arisen from the wearing away of the granite.

Turning our faces towards the direction from which we have come, a very pleasing view is presented. The little market town of South Brent is seen, with the lofty eminence which we have noticed, rising conspicuously above it. The vale of the Avon towards Avonwick, with the woods which cover the steep bank of the river, is plainly visible, and, as far as the eye can reach, are fields, with here and there a farmstead nestling amid the trees. On our right are the rocks on the summit of the Eastern Beacon, and near us on each hand several low, delapidated cairns.

Proceeding once more in a westerly direction, we shall observe at a short distance from the cross, a row of single upright stones intersecting the path nearly at right angles;

and a little further on, we shall again approach the row of stones which runs from Butterdon Hill towards Sharp Tor, and which here crosses our grassy track. This will now take us down a slope, and after passing the source of a rivulet that falls into the Erme, just below Harford, we shall soon reach the moor gate.

A walk of a few minutes will bring us to Harford Church, a little sanctuary pleasingly situated an the verge of the common. Here may be seen an altar tomb, on which is a brass with an effigy of a knight in complete armour. It represents Thomas Williams, Speaker of the House of Commons, in the reign of Elizabeth, and who died in 1566.

A mural monument will also be observed, erected by John Prideaux, to the memory of his parents, who were buried here. His father and mother are represented, with their twelve children, seven sons and five daughters. In the centre is the Bishop in his robes, and underneath is an inscription telling of him who rests below.

From Harford a path leads by the vicarage, and crossing Butter Brook by a single stone clapper, passes near the rugged pile of Tor Rocks. The road is regained just opposite the gate of Broomhill Farm, and a short distance further on it skirts the grounds of Lukesland, the pleasantly situated seat of Mr. James J. Mac Andrew. The mansion was built about forty years ago, close to the site of an older house, called Lukesland Grove, which was then pulled down. It presents an imposing appearance, and the grounds about it are so carefully laid out that a perfect harmony with the surroundings is preserved. Although standing some six hundred feet above sea level, the mansion, of which but a glimpse is obtainable from the road, is remarkably well sheltered.

Soon after passing the lodge gates of Lukesland, the more modern residence of Erme Wood will be observed on the right hand, and not far beyond this, just after commencing the descent of the hill, Stowford is reached. The old house has, in great part, disappeared, and the modern one has nothing in the shape of architectural beauties to recommend it. From Stowford we shall make our way to Ivybridge, the pleasing situation of which, and delightful surroundings, have combined to render it one of the most favourite resorts on the southern confines of the moor.

CHAPTER IV.

From the Erme to the Plym.

Ivybridge—The Erme—Church of St. John—Inscribed Stone—Fardle—Blatchford—Cornwood—Hawns and Dendles—Cross at Cholwich Town—An Ancient Farmhouse—Blackaton Cross—Cadaford Bridge.

Situated on the high road to Plymouth, from which town it is distant about eleven miles, and having a station on the Great Western Railway, Ivybridge is easily reached by the tourist, and there can be no better place from which to explore the extensive commons that fringe the South quarter of Dartmoor Forest.

The first object to claim our attention in this pleasant little town will be the old bridge spanning the river, and covered in great part with ivy, but whether it is the actual one whence the place derives its name is open to question. There is, however, not much doubt about its being the same that existed in Sir William Pole's day. That writer states that " Ivebrigge tooke its name from ye bridge which lieth over ye Erme beinge much inclined to the ivy,"* but as the village was known by the name it now bears long before his day, it would seem that the bridge took the place of a more ancient one. It is plainly noticeable from beneath, that at some period it has been widened. The original purpose of the bridge, that of affording the means of horses only crossing the stream, would not have necessitated the construction of one of the width of that now existing. With our modern ideas we should regard it as narrow, but we must not forget that there is some difference between what would be required for the passage of a pack-horse, and for a wheeled vehicle. It

---

* This was written in the early part of the seventeenth century, Sir William Pole dying in 1635.

is, however, of sufficient size for its present purpose, for about 1832 a new one was built a short distance below, and it is there the main road now crosses the stream, and consequently the former is relieved of most of the traffic. Four parishes meet at the old bridge, those on the eastern bank of the river being Ugborough and Harford, and those on the western, Ermington and Cornwood.

The Erme is a charming river, and to trace it to its source will prove, for one who is not afraid of a day's walk, a most delightful ramble. In order to do this he should proceed up the hill towards the railway station, and immediately after passing beneath the viaduct, a path will be observed on the right which leads directly to the river. The rambler will now find himself in Stowford Cleave, a deep winding valley whose precipitous sides are thickly clothed with trees, and running between Henlake and Hanger Downs, and a portion of Harford Moor. At each step new beauties will unfold themselves. Now the path is carried close to the river's brink, while a little further on the stream is lost in the thick and tangled foliage, to almost suddenly reappear at the head of some bend hitherto concealed by the dark firs. Here a deep pool, partly hidden by grey rocks, and above it an open reach, where the shallow waters run murmuringly over the pebbles. Above, the sky almost shut out from view by the living canopy of green; below, the feet sinking deeply in moss, and the tall ferns reaching nearly to one's waist, when for a moment the path is forsaken. The carolling of happy birds, the hum of insects, the gentle rustling of leaves and the sound of running waters, form fitting music to charm the ear and call forth from the heart of the contemplative man praises of nature's God. Anon the path becomes rougher, and in part obliterated, and by-and-bye the valley widens a little, and glimpses of the moor are obtained. Further on, the hills come in view, and up yonder, upon the very verge of the common, is the little church of Harford, with trees clustering about it, the whole picture at this point being as charming a one as it is possible to conceive. Still onward, the eyes of the rambler feasting upon the view before him till leaving the river for a small space, and crossing a field, he gains a lane that will lead him to Harford Bridge, upon the skirts of the moor. Here he will linger to observe the many fresh beauties around him, ere entering upon the commons, and bestow some notice upon the old structure thrown over the river. And now he will bid adieu to the fields and the woods, for the moor is before him. As he passes into its recesses he will meet with much that will afford him delight. Nature will be seen in her ruder form, while the cairn and the stone circle will speak of those who in the early days dwelt in the silent valley through which flows the beautiful stream.

Ivybridge Church is a modern building, having been opening in 1882, and it possesses but little to interest. The ruins of the old church close by are, however, very picturesque, being almost entirely covered with ivy, but can boast of no great antiquity, the original edifice only dating back to 1789, while some portion of what is now seen are the remains of additions made to it so late as 1835. Previous to an ecclesiastical district being formed out of the parishes of Ugborough, Ermington, and Cornwood, it was called St. John's Chapel, and was enlarged in the year just named, in consequence of the increase in the number of inhabitants. When the present church was built the old one was dismantled, but the tower and the walls were suffered to remain intact, adding much to the attractivness of the surroundings of the new edifice.

Near the lower end of the town, and lying considerably back from the road, is Highlands, the seat of Mr. William Coryton, and where formerly resided Mr. William Cotton, the founder of the Cottonian Library at Plymouth. Below it on the other side of the way, is the chapel of the Wesleyans, a remarkably fine building, and nearly opposite to this was formerly the chief hotel of the place. This is shown in an engraving in Moore's *History of Devon*, with the stage-coach ready to start at the door.

A road runs from Ivybridge to the town of Tavistock, passing through the village of Cornwood, where it is crossed by the one which we have already pointed out as the ancient track between Buckfast and Plympton. At the Plym the Tavistock road joins another, which is also very ancient, and which we shall notice later on, but for the present shall confine our attention to the road from Ivybridge to the stream named.

Leaving the old bridge over the Erme, we make our way up the hill by the side of the churchyard, and passing the substantial granite building erected for the accommodation of the Orphan Girls' School, founded by Dame Hannah Rogers, we shall soon reach a part of the road that runs parallel to the railway for a short distance. As we proceed we shall notice on our left some buildings a little way down the hill; these are the kennels of the Dartmoor hounds. Below them is Woodlands, a hamlet on the old Plymouth road, of which, according to Risdon, there were anciently lords bearing the same name, one of them—Walter Woodland—being servitor to the Black Prince. After passing the lane that leads down to this place we shall, at the distance of about three quarters of a mile, reach a small wood, which the road we are pursuing skirts for a hundred yards or so. From this a little rivulet issues, the roadway being carried over it by a bridge formed by stones being laid across its channel, but it is only of small size. It is known locally as Potsans Bridge, and though insignificant in itself, has yet some interest attaching to it, for it was here that the inscribed stone, generally referred to as the Fardle Stone, was found.

Its position in the bridge was at the lower end, a circumstance to which it owes its preservation, for had it been placed in the centre, it would either have been covered entirely by the road metalling, and so never have been discovered, or by being in the way of the traffic have suffered injury. It was taken from the bridge to Fardle farm-court, whence it was afterwards removed to the British Museum, through the instrumentality of Sir Edward Smirke. It is a matter for congratulation that so interesting a stone has been preserved, but at the same time one cannot but feel that it would have been more satisfactory had steps been taken to effect this without removing it far from the spot on which it was found. The stone, which Sir Edward described in an article in the *Transactions of the Royal Institution of Cornwall*, in 1861, is said to be six feet three inches in length, two feet ten inches in breadth, and to have a thickness of about seven inches.

The inscriptions upon this stone have been variously read. One side is said to bear the word *Sagranui*, and the other *Fanoni Maqvirini*,* both in the Roman character, while along

---

*Other renderings are *Sagramni*, and *Sapanui*, and in the second name *Maqvisini*. The *Maq* is equivalent to *Mac*, "the son of."

its edge is an Ogham inscription, † which has been given as *Safaqquci Maqiqici*, or possibly, *Maqirici*. Dr. Ferguson states that the Ogham inscriptions of South Britain are nearly always accompanied by a corresponding one in the Roman character. But this does not seem to be the case on the Fardle Stone, if the Oghams have been read correctly, the inscriptions appearing to be independent of each other, and commemorating three different persons, Sagramnus, and Fanonus, the son of Virinus (Fanon the son of Rian) in the Roman lettering, and Safaqquc, the son of Qici, or Cuic. The Fardle Stone and a stone at Tavistock are the only ones that have been found in Devon with an Ogham inscription, but they prove that the symbol of the ancient Irish language was in the far-away days not unknown in this part of our island.

---

† The characters of the Ogham alphabet, or symbols of the Erse, or ancient Irish language, are simply notches and short lines cut on or across an upright line, the latter being generally in the angle of the stone on which the inscription is graven, and the letters so formed are read upwards. If we imagine ourselves to be looking at a stone on which the alphabet is cut, we shall find it to be as follows. The angle of the stone shall form the *fleasg*, or upright line, and we must commence at the bottom.

One notch - - - - a	One line on the right of the upright line - - h
Two notches - - - o	Two lines - - d
Three „ - - - - u	Three „ - - t
Four „ - - - - e	Four „ „ - - k
Five „ - - - i	Five „ „ - - q
One line across the upright line - - - - m	One line on the left of the upright line „ - - b
Two lines „ - - g	Two lines - - l
Three „ „ - - ng	Three „ „ - - f
Four „ „ - - st	Four „ „ - - s
Five „ „ - - r	Five „ „ - - n

Prior to 1873 the sign for the letter B was not known, but in that year this was discovered, a stone now at Tavistock affording the requisite information. Dr. Ferguson of Dublin having taken a cast of this stone was able to decipher it on his return home, and the sign for B was ascertained without any doubt, as the stone bore the same inscription in the Roman character as it did in the Ogham.

It will be noticed that no letter is represented by more than five lines; this has been considered as suggestive of these signs having had their origin from such as could be readily made by the fingers.

Fardle was the ancestral home of the Raleighs, though Sir Walter himself was not born there, his father, either before, or soon after his first marriage, having left it for Hayes, in the parish of East Budleigh. Of the ancient house much still remains, including a portion of the chapel. It is now the property of Mr. J. D. Pode, of Slade, a charming seat about a mile or so distant.

Leaving Fardle, and passing over Houndle, or Houndale, Hill, we reach Moor Cross, where a road leads up on the right to Hanger Down, a common on the high ground between the valleys of the Erme and the Yealm. A visit to its breezy summit, where is a clump of trees, known as the Round Plantation, will well repay the rambler, the view it commands being extensive and of varied interest. At Moor Cross is an entrance to Blachford, which domain is for some distance skirted by the road we are now pursuing. Further on this is carried over the Yealm, which here leaves the noble deer-park, and pausing for a space upon the bridge, we may obtain a view of its timbered slopes. A short walk up a gentle ascent, with the park still stretching away on our right, and we shall reach the village of Cornwood, or, as it is locally called, Cross.

Whether a cross ever stood in this village, I have been unable to learn. Its local name may, or may not, indicate that such was the case, but apart from this there are considerations that render it not unlikely. As already stated, the road to Tavistock is here intersected by that running to Plympton from Buckfast, and which crossing the Erme at Harford Bridge, and leaving Blachford to the south, passes through the village at which we have arrived. It is therefore, more than probable that at the point where two such important roads crossed each other, a stone cross was once to be seen.

But although at present such does not exist, it is satisfactory to note that ere long this little village will have another claim to its homely appellation. It has been determined to erect a Latin cross in memory of Lord and Lady Blachford, from a design of Mr. James Hine. It is to be of granite raised in the parish, and will probably be executed by a Cornwood man, under Mr. Hine's supervision.

The church is Perpendicular in style with Early English chancel, and is dedicated to St Michael. It is pleasingly situated, at a short distance from the village, and the churchyard contains a number of grave stones with interesting epitaphs upon them. Built into the hedge by the roadside about a furlong south of the lich-gate, are several pieces of carved stone, the occurrence of which here may probably arouse the curiosity of the antiquary. But the Highway Board contractor is alone responsible for their present position. They were taken from the windows of the church, when the edifice was restored, and after lying for some time in the churchyard, were removed and utilized in the building of the hedge.

Cornwood is but a small place, but picturesque in appearance, and with surroundings possessing much interest. It is overlooked by the fine frontier height of Pen Beacon, one of the most prominent of the hills of Southern Dartmoor.

Within a short distance of the village is Hawns and Dendles, a thickly wooded valley, running up into the moor, down which the river Yealm flows over rocks and boulders of granite. It is deservedly renowned, its sylvan beauties constituting a powerful attraction for the visitor, and even on the borders of the moor not many spots will be found to surpass it. The name is certainly peculiar. Hawns is said to have been derived from a Madame Hawns, who, according to tradition, had a mansion somewhere in the valley, but as this rests upon a very shadowy foundation, little or no reliance can be placed upon the statement. Mr. J. D. Pode states that title deeds in his possession show that for more than a hundred years past the spelling of the name has not varied (except that an *e* is sometimes placed before the *s*), so that there seems to be little doubt that the present form is correct, whatever its meaning may be. The derivation of Dendles is a matter about which we can be more certain. Mr. Pode looked through some title deeds with the late Lord Blachford and found the name to be a corruption of Daniels.

Resuming our way we shall proceed towards Piall Bridge having on our left the grounds of Delamore, the seat of Admiral Parker, and at one time the residence of Winthrop Mackworth Praed, the poet. At a much earlier period the mansion, together with the manor of Cornwood, belonged to the Bellmains, to members of which family there is a monument in the church.

About half a mile beyond Piall Bridge we shall cross Quick's Bridge, and commence the ascent of the hill towards Tolch Moor Gate, the road being on the verge of a common. About midway we shall notice on our right hand a white gate, opening upon a private lane that leads to Cholwich Town, an ancient farmhouse, and the former seat of the Cholwich family. A short distance within this is an old granite cross which was first noticed several years ago by the Rev. W. C. Lukis in company with Mr. J. D. Pode, and was serving, as it does at present, as a gate post.

We shall find it to be a wayside cross of the rudest type, and as the greater part of each arm has been knocked off in order to adapt it to its meaner purpose, it might very well be passed without its real nature being discovered. That it was first put to its present use a long while since is evident, from the point of fracture of one of the arms being worn quite smooth.

There is little doubt that it originally stood by the side of the track on the line of which the road we have been following is now formed, and it is not unlikely that it was also intended to point the way to a fording-place on the stream at present crossed by Quick's Bridge.

The height of this cross is rather over five and a half feet, and it is nearly four feet in girth immediately below the arms or what remains of them. These are not quite opposite each other, there having been apparently little care expended in the fashioning of this ancient stone.

Cholwich Town farmhouse, which is about half a mile from the cross, presents a good example of the old-time moorland mansion. Though most of the extensive outbuildings have fallen to decay, being in great measure replaced by modern ones, and the site only of the chapel can now be seen, the dwelling itself remains much as it was in bygone days. Its outside appearance is marred by its having been found necessary to plaster the walls, but the old chambers with their granite arched doorways and mullioned windows, the roomy kitchen with its wide hearth, are still as of yore. Many years have passed since any of the Cholwich family dwelt in this "town place" under Pen Beacon, and but little is now known of them. It is said, but we know not with what truth, that its last representative died in prison.

Leaving Cholwich Town, we shall make our way to Tolch Moor Gate at the summit of the hill, and thence descend to the little bridge over the Torry near by. Crossing this we proceed towards Lee Moor House, with the evidences of the great china clay industry carried on in this part of the moor immediately around us. Passing the house, and the enclosures surrounding it, we shall shortly perceive another relic of the days when the road we are pursuing was probably little other than a green path, for beside the highway, on our right, we find an old stone cross. Near at hand a path leads across the common to the village of Shaugh, and we may not unreasonably suppose that its situation here was chosen not only for the purpose of marking the forerunner of the present road, but also of indicating the point where this branch diverged.

Rowe, in his *Perambulation of Dartmoor*, has a passing notice of this cross, "the shaft of which," he says, "appears to have been broken off, as there is only enough now left to raise the cross slightly above the large block in which a socket has been formed to receive it." Since this was written, however, it has been placed upon a shaft, and properly fixed in the socket, and now stands erect. Through having been misinformed, I was led to attribute this praiseworthy act to a nobleman who we can well believe would have undertaken it had the matter been brought to his notice. But I have since found that the restoration of this cross was effected by one with whom my father was many years ago associated in religious work on this part of Dartmoor—Mr. Phillips, formerly of Lee Moor. The stone now forming the shaft was originally cut for a window-sill, which accounts for one of its corners only being bevelled.

The cross is five feet ten inches in height, and two feet across the arms; the block in which the socket is cut is about fourteen inches in thickness, and is circular in shape, its diameter being about three and a half feet.

In my first notice of this cross I stated that it had been suggested to me that the name by which it was known in the neighbourhood—Roman's Cross—had become attached to it in consequence of its being usually referred to as the Roman cross, the term at length becoming a proper name. I also said that it had occurred to me that this may originally have been Rumon, one of the saints to whom the Abbey of Tavistock was dedicated, and that pilgrims journeying over this road to the abbey may have bestowed the saint's name upon the cross. When I wrote this I had never heard, or seen, such a derivation of the name suggested, nor was I by any means convinced of its correctness. I find it stated, however, in a paper read before the members of the Plymouth Institution in 1889, six years after my account of the cross first appeared, that " it has been suggested *by several*," not only that it derived its name from St. Rumon, but that it was once dedicated to him. I have not met with such suggestions in the pages of any writer, and I now believe the idea to be wrong.

Since the first appearance of my account of this cross I have greatly extended my enquiries in its vicinity and have spent much time on and around Lee Moor. I have there found not only this cross, but others in the neighbourhood, referred to constantly as the Roman, or Roman's cross, meaning the Roman Catholic cross, and I am convinced that the suggestion which traces the origin of the name to this is correct and that it has nothing whatever to do with the saint. All the older people on that side of the moor speak of the cross as Blackaton Cross, and this is the name that will now be found on the latest Ordnance Map. It takes its name from a slight depression near by, where much peat has been cut, and which is known to the moor people as Blackaton Slaggets.

Mention must not be omitted of another object in the neighbourhood bearing a name similar to that bestowed upon the cross. This is an excavation known as the Roman Camp, but which investigation has shown to be nothing of the kind. Mr. J. Brooking Rowe's idea that it was a reservoir for water nad is of comparatively modern construction, certainly commends itself as being highly probable.

A tradition affirms that Blackaton Cross was erected to mark the spot where St. Paul once preached, and we shall probably not be sceptical regarding it *when* it is proved to our satisfaction that St Paul ever set foot in Britain. In the name of the stream which rises below Cholwich Town, the

Blackaton Cross.

Piall Brook, it is, perhaps, not unlikely that we see the origin of the story of the saint's presence in the locality, such being invariably called Pall by the moor people.

Many rude stone remains are to be found in the vicinity of Blackaton Cross, but the spoliator has unfortunately been at work among them. An upright stone will be seen on the higher ground to the north-west. This is Emmett's Post, a modern shaft, serving to mark the boundary between the lands of Lord Morley and Sir Massey Lopes.

The view from Blackaton Cross embraces an extensive range of the cultivated country to the south and south-west, bounded by the Channel; while to the north and north-east are seen numerous hills with their granite crests. Brent Tor is a conspicuous object far away to the northward, while the rocky piles of Great and Little Trowlsworthy Tors rise near at hand.

We pass onward and descend the hill to the Plym, where at Cadaford Cridge, we shall find that our road, as already stated is joined by another. This as we shall presently see is formed on the line of an ancient track leading from Plympton to Tavistock, by way of Meavy and Sampford Spiney. To the first named town we shall therefore make our way in order that we may trace the road from its commencement there, and thus shall again reach the banks of the Plym at this point, but by another route.

CHAPTER V.

The Via Crucis of the Augustine Canons.

Hemerdon Ball—Plympton St. Maurice—Plympton Castle—The Priory—Church of Plympton St. Mary—Cross by the Torry—Browney Cross—Base of Cross at Beatland Corner—Shaugh Cross—Shaugh Church—The White Thorn—The Dewerstone—Cross near Shaden Brake—Cross near Cadaford Bridge—Lynch Down—Marchants Cross.

The road from Cornwood to Plympton, it is more than probable, takes nearly the same route as the old track which we have already referred to as running westward from Buckfast, and which we entered upon at Spurrell's Cross. It again becomes our path, and will conduct us from Cornwood to Lutton, whence we shall follow it through Sparkwell, a hamlet in Plympton St. Mary parish, close to which are Goodamoor and Beechwood, and a little to the west of it Hemerdon, three seats delightfully placed in well-wooded grounds. On our right, but hidden from view by the trees, rises the eminence known as Hemerdon Ball, on the summit of which is a plantation, forming a conspicuous object in the landscape for many miles round. The slopes of the hill, which is at the extremity of a spur of the moor, are now cultivated.

Passing Hemerdon we descend West Park Hill, and noticing the substantial farmhouse of Old Newnham near its foot, and the lodge at the entrance to the modern residence, shall soon after turn into a lane on the left. This will conduct us to the higher part of Ridgway, whence a walk of a few minutes will bring us to Plympton St. Maurice, otherwise Plympton Earl.

Here near the south porch of the church is a very fine cross, the ancient shaft of which has a not uninteresting history. It owes its preservation to Mr. J. Brooking Rowe, a painstaking and trustworthy antiquary, who has done a great deal in the direction of furnishing us with historical accounts of the religious foundations in the county, and who has industriously collected much information relative to Plympton history. In 1861 alterations were made to the old Guildhall, when this shaft was found built into a wall separating the court from the lock-up, or clink, and which it is supposed was built in 1680. Mr. Rowe caused this interesting memorial of old Plympton to be removed to the Churchyard, where it was placed close to the tower, and there it remained until the last year of the nineteenth century. That year saw its restoration, and on the 27th November the re-dedication of the cross took place.

The shaft, in the top of which an iron dowell was fixed and so firmly as to resist all attempts to remove it, was upwards of nine feet high. On this a new head was placed and the cross set upon a fine octagonal base of granite of three steps, and three feet in height. The foot of the shaft is square, but a short distance up the corners are chamfered, the octagonal form thus produced, elegantly tapering. It will be noticed that one of the chamfers has been broken away and the surface smoothed. This, it is supposed, was done when it was built into the wall, of which it formed part of the face. Mr. Rowe conjectures it to have been the market cross, and its approximate date to be 1380.

The restoration of the Plympton Cross has been most satisfactorily carried out, a great deal of care and thought having been bestowed upon it. It is striking in appearance, and all who take an interest in the preservation of our antiquities will be gratified at seeing in this ancient market town an object so much in keeping with the surroundings.

At the re-dedication service there were appropriate prayers and hymns, and an address was delivered by the Bishop of Crediton.

The Church is dedicated to St. Thomas of Canterbury, but is more commonly known as St. Maurice, from the chantry chapel in the south aisle, founded by John Brackley, towards the close of the fourteenth century. The second name of the place—Plympton Earl—is derived from the ancient Earls of Devon, who were formerly its lords.

Plympton as one of the four stannary town of Devon, and as an old borough once returning members to Parliament, is interesting, while the remains of the Norman castle and the many ancient buildings in the town render it doubly so. The castle was built by Richard de Redvers, upon whom

Henry I. bestowed the barony of Plympton, and also created him Earl of Devon, and it was long the seat of the family. Baldwin, the second earl, took up arms against Stephen, and while defending the city of Exeter, it is stated that those who were holding Plympton Castle, surrendered to the king. Baldwin was banished, but afterwards returning, was reinstated. During the civil war Prince Maurice, while beseiging the town of Plymouth, made the castle his headquarters. Little more than a portion of the keep, upon a mound, now remains, but viewed from the entrance to the churchyard, it is a picturesque object, the huge fragments of massive wall being partially covered with ivy. The quaint old topographer Leland refers to it as "a faire large castelle and dungeon, whereof the waulles yet stonde, but the logginges within be decayed." On the castle mound some years since was found a bronze coin of Ferdinandus II., Grand Duke of Etruria, whose son Cosmo III. landed at Plymouth, in April 1669, and made a tour of some months through England. A building worthy of notice is the Grammar School, built in 1664, Elize Hele, of Fardle, having left a sum of money for its foundation. The father of the celebrated Sir Joshua Reynolds was master of the school, and his son received some portion of his education here. Here, too, some ninety years later, in the first decade of the nineteenth century, was educated the Rev. Samuel Rowe, the author of the *Perambulation of Dartmoor*, a work involving a deal of research and evincing the great love he bore for that "wild and wondrous region."

Plympton House, a fine mansion of the time of Queen Anne, is now used as a private lunatic asylum.

The guildhall is a quaint building with an old-time air about it ; its front projects over the pavement and is supported upon arches.

The old Maudlin House is frequently referred to in the parish registers, one of the entries being as follows :

"1618 May 24 was buryed Charles Ffysher wch dyed within the pishe of Plympton Erell in the house over right against the Maudling house."

Another entry sets forth that on the 20th May 1613,

"Was buryed a walking woman wch dyed in a ffeeld between Plimpton Marie and Cornwood."

This event had a sad parallel in 1891, when a poor woman lost her life near Sparkwell, in the blizzard of March of that year. She was found lying in the snow, only a few yards from her door.

We cannot leave the town of Plympton without a feeling of regret, its old-world appearance and associations so impressing us that we hesitate to break the spell which a long lingering by its venerable buildings casts upon us.

The parish of Plympton St. Mary adjoins, and towards its church, which is very near, we now bend our steps. On entering the churchyard we shall observe a modern cross, at the western end of the building. This is a memorial to the Rev. Merton Smith, a former vicar of the parish, who lost his life in 1883, in the Pyrenees. The cross is of fine proportions, and stands upon a handsomely worked base, on a pedestal consisting of five steps, and octagonal in shape. It is a good example of the modern sculptor's art.

The church is large, and contains several monuments. Its style is a mixture of Decorated and Perpendicular, and in addition to the two side aisles, there are two exterior aisles. The groining in the roof of the south porch will not fail to arrest the attention of the visitor upon entering.

The legend so frequently attached to ecclesiastical buildings, of the arch enemy of man having removed the stones from the site on which it was originally intended to erect the edifice is related of this church, which the tradition states would not have been placed in so low a situation but for this.

In a little work by the Rev. W. I. Coppard, vicar of the parish, entitled *Cottage Scenes during the Cholera*, we read that at a vestry meeting held on the 13th January, 1833, the year after the visitation of the cholera, it was resolved:

"That a small stone, in the shape of a cross, with the date 1832 engraved upon it, be placed as a memorial at the head of all the graves of persons who had died of the awful disease of cholera."

A priory of Augustine Canons formerly existed at Plympton, founded by Bishop Warlewast, who in 1121 suppressed a College of the Benedictine order, that had been founded here by one of the Saxon kings. Baldwin de Redvers of the castle endowed it, and it became one of the wealthiest foundations in the county, its revenue being even greater than that of the rich abbey of Tavistock.

Among the possessions of the priory were the manors of Shaugh, Meavy, and Sampford Spiney, and the monks' road to those places, as we shall shortly see, was marked by a line of crosses. It runs over the moor and extends to Tavistock, and though not the most direct route from Plympton to that town, we can readily understand, as it passed through the abbey manors, was the one generally used by the brothers of the priory when they desired to visit the great Benedictine house on the Tavy. The monks of the latter probably also often used it when journeying to Plympton or to their manor of Plymstock; indeed, there is every probability that in early times it was a much frequented track.

With the object of examining the crosses on it, it will be necessary that we trace the road to Tavistock, but for the present we shall follow it only to the village of Meavy. We therefore, leave the church of St. Mary and make our way up the right bank of the Torry, a stream rising on the moor under Pen Beacon, and which we crossed near its source, when on our way to Lee Moor.

At Plympton it is spanned by two bridges, one near the church we have just been noticing, and the other a short distance further up. A few yards below the latter, and in the bed of the little river, but quite close to its left bank is the shaft of a cross fixed into a socket-stone. The former is almost covered with vegetation, and were it not that the outer side of the square block of granite in which the socket is cut has escaped being overgrown through the water constantly washing it, the whole would be undiscernible. This stone, and even the shaft of the cross itself, is partly built into a garden wall that abuts on the river. The head and arms of the cross are gone. The shaft is very similar in shape to that of the Plympton St. Maurice Cross, though it is not of so great a height, but it is probable that a portion of it has been broken off. It is five feet three inches high, and at the bottom where it fits into the socket is square. The corners are, however, chamfered almost close down to the stone, so that it is really octagonal, the sides of this figure measuring five and a half inches each. The socket-stone has been carefully worked. It is twenty-one inches high and four feet long, but being built into the wall its exact breadth cannot be seen; its upper edges are bevelled.

The situation of this cross on the very verge of a stream would seem to point to its having marked a fording-place.

leading directly to the priory, the ancient bridge, if there was one here, probably occupying a different site from the present structure near by. But however this may be, it is certain that the old track we are about to follow started from this point, or very near it.

Leaving the Torry we take the road that passes through Colebrook, which place is close by. Here we shall notice a school and chapel belonging to the Methodist Free Church, the memorial stones of which, as the inscriptions on them testify, were laid by Mrs. Joseph Crossing, of Plymouth, that of the former in 1866, and the other in 1868. Our road turns up on the left, and soon after leaving the village we shall reach a spot where the lane branches. We pursue the one on the right, the left leading to Boringdon, the former seat of the Parker family, the present Earls of Morley; it is now used as a farm-house, and is a fine building, occupying a commanding situation. A little further on we obtain glimpses of Newnham and Elfordleigh, both surrounded by beautifully wooded grounds, and crossing the valley in which the latter stands, shall skirt Boringdon Wood. On reaching the top of the hill we perceive we are nearing the moor, several hills lying immediately before us, prominent among which we soon discover the crest of the Dewerstone Hill, near Shaugh. On our left, though not visible from the road, is Castle Ring, sometimes called Boringdon Camp, an ancient enclosure of about four acres in extent, and having traces of a ditch on the outside of the rampart.

Near an old granite post by the roadside we again commence to descend, and soon cross the tram-road that runs from below the Laira Bridge to the clay works on Lee Moor, and then having mounted a gentle ascent, shall reach the first of the objects of which we are in search.

This is Browney Cross, and in the old days when the wayfarer passed over this road it not only assured him that he was pursuing the right path to Tavistock or Shaugh, but also indicated where he was to turn off should he desire to go to Bickleigh. Now, a modern finger-post has taken its place, and the old cross has disappeared. All that remains to mark its site is the socket-stone in which it was fixed, and a ruined foundation. This stone is in the centre of a large, open space, covered with turf, and is now somewhat weathered. It is octagonal in shape, and measures four feet across the centre, and is over a foot thick. The socket that received the shaft is not quite square, being fifteen inches by thirteen, and about nine inches deep. The stone lies on a mound, and originally stood upon an elevated octagon, as is shown by four large stones close to it. These have been roughly hewn into shape, and it would seem that there must originally have been eight of them, forming a foundation of about eight feet across, so that there would be a step of about two feet in width around the socket stone. The latter has evidently not been moved away from its place, although the despoilers of this interesting memorial have partly raised it from its bed.

Not very far off to the E.N.E. is Collard Tor, and Pen Beacon with Shell Top rising behind it are also prominent objects in the view. In the opposite direction the eye rests upon the woods of Mount Edgcumbe, and looking nearly north-west, the pinnacles or Bickleigh church tower can be seen, peeping over the hill two miles away. Bickleigh is not strictly speaking a Dartmoor parish, that is to say, no part of it lies upon the moor, but it is nevertheless in the Dartmoor country, and it will be necessary for us to visit it, as there is a very fine cross in the village. But this we shall do later on, when we come to examine another group of crosses, and for that purpose shall return to this ancient way-mark. At present we leave it and pass up the lane to Niel Gate.

Here we enter upon the moor, which the road skirts for some distance. But we shall not now pursue it very far, for upon reaching the further corner of a plantation, and within a quarter of a mile of the gate, we shall find that a road diverges to Shaugh, and we shall turn a little from our way in order to visit that village. The point we have reached is known as Beatland Corner—usually called Binlin's Corner—and here formerly stood another of the crosses marking the tract we have been following from Plympton, and also indicating the point at which the wayfarer should leave it, if journeying to Shaugh. Now, all that is to be seen is the base, or stone in which the shaft was fixed. It stands on the verge of the common, close by the road, and is very nearly two feet square. The socket, which is not now quite intact, the edge of the stone being broken, is very large, being fifteen inches by twelve, and is seven inches deep. There is no trace of the

Shaugh Cross.

cross near it, but one that we shall presently notice possesses a shaft that would have fitted this socket. As, however, the stone is over three-quarters of a mile distant, it may perhaps not be considered very probable, that it ever belonged to this base. We shall refer to this again when we come to examine it.

A walk of about half a mile will bring us to Shaugh, immediately on entering which we shall see, close to the gate, of the new vicarage, and some short distance to the east of the church, a very good specimen of a cross. It stands in the hedge, being fixed in a socket-stone some three and a half feet wide, and eight or nine inches thick, and is somewhat out of the perpendicular. One of the arms is slightly fractured, but otherwise this old cross is in a very fair state of preservation. It is about five and a half feet high, the shaft having a width of one foot, but it is not quite square, being a little less than that in thickness. The arms measure two feet across, and are about ten inches deep. The corners have been chamfered, but owing to the wearing of the granite this is not immediately discernible, except at the arms. This old cross is a pleasing object, its rude fashioning harmonizing well with its surroundings, where everything speaks to us of the moor. Here is the substantially built church, that has so long withstood the fury of the blasts that often sweep down upon it from the rock-crowned hill behind; and here the little cottages, reared near the rugged slope, with glimpses between them of grey rocks and patches of fern and gorse.

In Shaugh Church, which dates back to the time of Henry VI., is a very beautiful font cover. This, it appears, had been removed from the church while it was undergoing restoration in 1868 and 1869, and placed in a loft at a neighbouring farm. The Rev. Prebendary Bartholomew having called attention in 1878 to the fact of its existence, the Rev. J. B. Strother, at that time vicar of the parish, made enquiries, and discovered it. It was in a damaged state, and has been most carefully restored. It is of oak, and between eight and nine feet in height, and octagonal in plan. The sides of the two lower stages are perpendicular, but the upper one is of a spiral form. It is surmounted by the figure of a mitred bishop.

Opposite the church is the village inn, the White Thorn, where formerly was to be seen a peat fire that had not been extinguished for a great number of years. I remember the landlord telling me in 1873, that he had then been living there over twenty years, and that he had kept it burning during that time, and his predecessor had told him that for a similar period he also had not suffered it to go out.

A road leads from the village down the steep side of the common to Shaugh Bridge, the romantic surroundings of which have earned for it a more than local fame. Its neighbourhood was a favourite resort of the poet Carrington, who in some charming lines has pictured it at the close of a beautiful summer day.

Retracing our steps, or, if we choose, taking an alternative route from the village, we regain the road, and resume our walk, with the enclosed country on the left. On nearing a grove of trees we shall observe, reared against the hedge of Shaden Brake, what appears to be a short cross, but which is really the upper portion of a large one. For years it lay on the ground, and formed the bottom stone of a stile formerly at this place. It is of very rude workmanship, and measures three feet from the top of the head to where the shaft is fractured, but there are probably some three or four feet of the latter missing. It is twenty-two inches across the arms, which spring some four inches from the shaft, and one of these is broken. It is this cross that I suggest may have belonged to the base we examined at Beatland Corner. The shaft would just fit the socket, it being nearly fifteen inches wide, and about nine inches thick. It is true that some little distance now separates them, but there are instances of crosses on the moor, and on its borders, having been removed even further from their original position; the cross at Sheepstor is an instance, and another is afforded by a cross on Terhill, in the south quarter of the forest. The measurements seem to lend colour to the supposition, as also does the style of workmanship, the cross and the socket-stone both being of a rude type.

Shortly after passing the cross we commence the descent towards the Plym, on reaching which we meet the road we have already traced from Ivybridge and Cornwood.

We shall cross the stream by the bridge, about the true name of which there seems to be some uncertainty. Cadaford is the usually accepted form now, though it is frequently called Cadover, which is merely a corruption of the former. The farm near by is called Cadworthy, and the bridge, without doubt, is named after the settlement, or " weorthig," that preceded the present homestead. More than six hundred years ago there was a bridge here, probably a clapper, as is proved by an ancient deed, to which we shall have occasion later on to refer. Several places and objects in this part of the moor are mentioned in it, and among them the " ponte de Cadaworthy." It is easy to see how this would become corrupted to the present form of the name.

Making our way up the slope of Wigford Down, to the left of the road and in a north-westerly direction, we shall find near the hedge a portion of what must have been an exceedingly fine cross. It was discovered lying near here by the soldiers encamped in the vicinity, during the Autumn Manœuvres in 1873, and was set up by them at the request of the Rev. G. R. Scobell, then vicar of Shaugh. It was placed on the centre of a small grassy mound, rather more than nine feet in diameter, and surrounded by a little trench. The greater part of the shaft is gone, but the portion now remaining measures from the surface of the ground to the top about two and a half feet, and across the arms it is two feet five inches. The width of the shaft below the arms is thirteen inches, and from the upper surface of the arms to the top of the shaft it is exactly twelve inches. The shaft tapers from the arms upward; below them it appears to have had its sides parallel.

On one face of this cross there is a fracture, a piece being split off from it, but its other is uninjured. Here are three incised crosses; one on each arm, and the third, a little larger than the others, in the centre, exactly where the arms intersect the shaft. There are faint traces of what seem to be incised crosses on the fractured side, but they cannot be determined as such with certainty.

The last time I saw this cross, in 1901, it had been thrown down. This was probably done by cattle rubbing against it, and unless it is provided with a socket stone it will not be easy to guard against its overthrow.

While this cross served to mark the track to Tavistock from Plympton and from Cornwood, it also pointed out the

CHAPTER VI.

The Crosses of Meavy.

The Meavy Oak—A Missing Village Cross—Its Discovery and Restoration—Meavy Church—Cross in Wall of Transept—Tomb of Lady Seccombe—Tomb of Walter Mattacott—Gratton—Chapel of St. Matthew—Greenwell Down—Greenwell Girt—Base of a Wayside Cross—Urgles—Wigford Down—An Old Path.

Having followed the Monk's road from Plympton to the Mew, and noticed the crosses by which it was marked, we shall leave it for the present in order to visit Meavy, which, was one of the possessions of Plympton Priory.

From the cross at the foot of Lynch Hill we proceed to Marchants Bridge near at hand, beneath which flows the Mew as it emerges from its leafy screen, and crossing it shall make our way by a lane to the little village.

Here, a most pleasing picture meets our view. An open green, with a noble old oak, whose boughs, as though to protect it, are flung over an ancient granite cross, reared almost close to its trunk; and quite near to both, the gate of that sacred spot where

"The rude forefathers of the hamlet sleep."

The trunk of the tree is hollow, and in a note to Carrington's poem of *Dartmoor*, published in 1826, it is stated on the authority of the hostess of the village inn, that nine persons once dined in the cavity. Though it is now but a mere shell, yet the branches put forth their leaves in due season, and it is to be hoped that the day is far distant when the shadow of "Meavy's venerable oak" shall cease to fall across the village green.

For more than a hundred years the Meavy cross was missing from its place beneath the tree. Whither it had disappeared no man knew, but the base and pedestal told where it once had been. That it would ever be discovered and set up in its old place was imagined by none; but that this was at length the case, all who are interested in the preservation of our antiquities will rejoice to learn.

To a former rector, the Rev. W. A. G. Gray, do we owe this, for it was his kindly hand that rescued the cross from the ignoble position whence it had been banished, and restored it to its rightful place. About the year 1882 he found it, or rather the shaft, for the head and arms had been broken off, in one of the glebe fields, where it was serving as a gate-post. But its true character was easy recognizable, and causing a fresh tenon to be cut so that it might fit into the socket of the base upon the green, it was once more erected under the sheltering boughs of the ancient oak. Like the pedestal it is octagonal, and of a beautiful tapering form. The oldest man in the parish, who was then about ninety years of age, and who possessed a remarkably clear recollection of all parish matters, had been unable to give any information respecting its whereabouts, nor had he ever heard his father speak of it. It is therefore nearly certain that more than a century had elapsed since the time this cross was removed from its pedestal, and the probability is that the period was much longer. When found there were six holes in it, one being filled with lead, in which some gate fastenings had evidently been fixed, and the disposition of these showed that the stone had been made use of as a gate-post in more than one position.

For a considerable time the pedestal upon which the base of the cross stood, consisted of two steps only, formed by eleven blocks of hewn granite, there being six in the lower one, and five in the upper. The sides of the octagon were not equal, varying from about twenty-eight inches to forty-five in the lower step, and it was evident that the stones had been moved from their proper positions, The lower stage was about nine feet in diameter, and about fifteen or sixteen inches high. On the upper stage was placed the octagonal base, which is twenty-two inches high, and sloping at the top. The shaft of the cross was five and a half feet high, and at its foot was just over four feet in girth.

When, in 1895, the complete restoration of the cross was decided upon it was discovered that there were other stones in existence similar in form to those composing the calvary on the green. Investigation showed that they had certainly belonged to it, and that originally it had consisted of three steps. These were brought back to their old place, and the pedestal was re-set, very little new work requiring to be introduced. A new head was made for the shaft by a stonemason of Walkhampton, and the restoration was complete. Antiquaries will feel grateful to Mr. Gray for this good work, as indeed will all to whom the sight in our villages of these memorials of the years that are flown is a source of pleasure.

Entering the churchyard, we shall notice that there is a small granite cross over the porch, and one also on the roof of the aisle, and another over the transept. Immediately above the window of the latter is a niche in the wall, reaching to its apex, in which is a slab bearing upon it a cross in relief. The church is of the fifteenth century, but portions of it remain which are of earlier date, the north pillar of the chancel-arch exhibiting traces of Norman carving.

In a corner of the churchyard is a monument erected over the grave of Lady Seccombe, of Walreddon, who died in 1884, consisting of a beautiful white marble cross and pedestal; and nearer to the lich-gate is a squared granite block on which an inscription is cut in relief. This marks the grave of one Walter Mattacot, and the letters on the stone tells us that he died in 1657.

In the courtyard of Gratton Farm, in this parish, there was formerly a stone with an incised cross. This probably belonged to the old manor house there, though if it could be proved that the chapel of St. Matthew, licensed in 1433, the site of which is now unknown, stood anywhere near, we might be right in supposing it to be a relic of that building.

Reluctantly leaving Meavy, with its Elizabethan manorhouse, its time-worn cross, its granite tower and pleasant green, and its venerable oak, which tradition tells us was standing prior to the time when its lands were held by Judhael the Norman, we pass on our way to the extensive commons occupying the southern portion of the parish. The road at the western end of the village will lead us to a picturesque old bridge of one arch thrown across the Mew, whence by a true Devonshire lane we shortly reach a cross-road, and turning up the hill, shall enter upon Calisham Down.

Following the path that skirts this down, and passing through a gate we soon find ourselves on another common. This is Greenwell Down, across which we shall make our way, keeping close to the enclosures on our left, and shall strike a branch of the road that we have just forsaken, where it crosses an old working of the tin-miners, known as Greenwell Girt. Its sides are so overgrown with heather and fern that it would almost appear to one unaccustomed to viewing the remains of the old tinners' operations to be a naturally formed combe. It acts as a dividing line between Greenwell Down and Wigford Down, and can be traced for a considerable distance. It is carried down the hill towards Hooe Meavy, the lower part being planted with trees, forming a delightful avenue, and now known as Shady Combe.

Crossing this extensive working, we shall observe on a bank, close by the way, a stone that once supported a cross. In shape it is octagonal, but it is rather rudely cut. Four of its sides are perpendicular, the others slightly sloping. It is three feet across, and its greatest thickness is sixteen inches. This can be seen, as the low bank has slipped from beneath a part of it, so that it overhangs the side of the road, above which it is raised some four feet. The socket is five inches deep, and is very nearly square, being eleven and a half inches by ten and a half. As there is a hedge on the other side of the road that encloses some cultivated land, it is not unlikely that the cross which was once fixed on this old base was removed from its position to do duty as a gate-post.

Proceeding for a short distance we shall notice a rough track on our right, and striking into this shall cross the common in a south-westerly direction and so regain the road by which we entered on the down. This we shall follow until nearly reaching the gate that leads off the moor to Goodameavy. Here, by the roadside and opposite the gate of Urgles Farm, is the base of a cross. It is a large flat stone, about a foot thick, not exactly circular, its edge in one place being broken, which gives it something of a kidney shape. Its greatest diameter is five feet. The socket that received the shaft is not quite in the centre. It measures eleven inches by nine, and is very shallow, being only a little over four inches in depth. There is no trace of the cross, nor have I been able to learn that anyone has ever seen it.

In the preceding chapter we referred to a track over Wigford Down. This exists in the form of a green path, and may be followed from the cross near Cadaford Bridge to Urgles. Whatever the original purpose of the cross at the latter place may have been, it seems certain that one of its uses at all events was to indicate the direction of this path, and to point to the ford, or bridge, at Goodameavy, in the valley below. The road leads to Roborough Down and Buckland Abbey, and like the one we have traced from Plympton Priory, was doubtless often traversed by the monks in the days—

> "Ere yet, in scorn of Peter's-pence,
> And number'd bead and shrift,
> Bluff Harry broke into the spence
> And turn'd the cowls adrift."

In our progress across Wigford Down we shall have been gratified with the varied and extensive view that is commanded from it. The whole of the western fringe of the southern portion of Devon, extending from Plympton to Brent Tor is visible, backed by a wide range embracing the principal hills of East Cornwall. In the other direction a fine sweep of moor is presented, with many a noble tor uplifting its granite head, and looking down grimly on the smiling border valleys.

CHAPTER VII.

Crosses on the Lands of Amicia, Countess of Devon.

Bickleigh Vale—Maynstone Cross—Woolwell Cross—Bickleigh Cross—The Church—Socket Stone—Copris Cross—Buckland Abbey—Buckland Monachorum Cross—Shaft of Cross on Crapstone Farm—Horrabridge—Smalacumbe Cross—Sheepstor Cross—A Moorland Church—An Ancient Church House—The Pixies' Cave—The Path of the Monks.

In the lower valley of the Tavy, where the ground slopes gently to the river beneath the hanging woods, there rose in the later years of the thirteenth century a stately pile of buildings. When the workmen had completed their task, and the sounds of their tools were no longer heard, those whose future home it was to be, a colony of Cistercian monks, took up their abode there, and for the first time the hymn of praise resounded within the walls of Buckland Abbey.

This house was founded by Amicia, Countess of Baldwin de Redvers, Earl of Devon, who endowed it with certain lands, including three manors in the neighbourhood—Buckland, Bickleigh and Walkhampton. The foundation deed was signed by Amicia in the eighth of Edward I. (1280), and eleven years later the gift was confirmed by her daughter, Isabella de Fortibus, by charter. In these instruments the bounds of the lands bestowed upon the abbey are set forth, and among the various objects by which they were defined are named six crosses. These are given as Crucem Siwardi, Smalacumbacrosse, Yanedonecrosse, Maynstoncrossa, Crucem de Wolewille and Copriscrosse. The first will claim our attention when we come to describe the crosses on the Abbot's Way; for the present we shall confine our remarks to the others, noticing at the same time those which still exist within the boundaries of the manors of the countess.

We shall therefore now return to Browney Cross, which we may best do from Urgles by following the green path to Cadaford Bridge, and retracing our steps over the Plympton road. Arrived at the cross we turn into the lane leading to

Bickleigh, and passing Lower Whiteyborough, where is a cottage and a smithy, shall gain the crest of the next hill and thence descend to Bickleigh Bridge.

Close to this is the entrance to Bickleigh Vale, the charms of which have been sung by Nathaniel Howard, sometime schoolmaster at Tamerton Foliot, and a happy wooer of the muse. Near the lower end of the vale, and above the right bank of the river, is Mainstone Wood, the name of which favours the supposition that in, or near it, the boundary cross of the Countess Amicia bearing that name formerly stood.

But this cannot be determined with certainty. Indeed, it would appear from the foundation deed that this cross should be looked for to the east of the river, rather than on its western side. That it existed somewhere in this locality we may be sure, but many of the names on the deed cannot be positively identified, so that it becomes impossible to determine its exact situation.

The name would seem to indicate that the cross replaced an ancient menhir (*maen-stone*), or that it was simply incised upon the monolith, or rudely fashioned out of it.

With regard to the next cross mentioned on the deed, we can locate it with a greater degree of certainty. The boundary is drawn from Horyngbrok to the Plym "et ad Willebroke et ad crucem deWolewille," so that the river, and the brook separating the parishes of Bickleigh and Egg Buckland, and which rises not far from the farm of Woolwell, are clearly set forth. We are therefore able to fix the site of the cross near this farm, and that it was on the present Tavistock road is more than probable, since not only is that the situation in which it would be likely to be placed, but the words of the deed also lead us to suppose it. There the boundary is conterminous with the road as at present, and is drawn from Woolwell to Copriscrosse. The latter we shall presently notice.

As an endeavour to discover Maynstone Cross, or the one formerly at Woolwell, would only end in disappointment, we shall resume our walk to Bickleigh, and having mounted the steep hill leading from the bridge, shall shortly reach the village, where on the green and within a few yards of the churchyard gate, we shall find, if not one of the objects of our quest, one that will at least interest us.

Of Dartmoor and its Borderland.

Bickleigh Cross is in appearance striking, being well placed, and mounted on a calvary, consisting of two steps. The lower one is a square of six feet, formed by four granite stones, each constituting a side. The upper step is constructed somewhat differently, the stones, of which there are three only, being laid side by side. Its surface is about two-and-a-half feet from the ground, and on this rests the socket-stone, which is twenty-five inches square at the bottom. This has a plinth nine inches in height, the portion of the stone above being hollowed out to within a few inches of the top, the upper edge being bevelled; the surface in which the socket to receive the cross is cut, is thus reduced to a square of fifteen inches. All this, however, as well as the shaft of the cross itself, is of comparatively modern date compared to the head, which it is plainly to be seen is of some considerable antiquity, and it is a matter for congratulation that so much care has been taken to preserve this memorial of the old days. The shaft is thirteen inches square at the bottom, and of tapering form. It is nearly six feet high, and around the top is a fillet. The head which has been carefully fixed, rises twenty-eight inches above this fillet, and in addition to having been broken off from its original shaft, it has also sustained other injuries. Remains of much ornamentation in the angles of this cross, prove it to have been a very handsome one. The arms and top of the head are octagonal in shape.

Bickleigh Church was re-built in 1838, by Sir Ralph Lopes, of Maristowe, the patron of the living. In the old edifice was a monument to the memory of Nicholas Slanning, who was killed in a duel with John (afterwards Sir John) Fitz, in 1599. Portions of this monument, which was in a very dilapidated condition, were preserved at the time the church was rebuilt, but previous to its demolition a drawing of it, with a copy of the inscriptions it bore, was made by the Rev. W. I. Coppard, of Plympton.

The tower is ancient, and is surmounted by large crocketted pinnacles, and possesses a corner turret.

From Bickleigh we shall take the road which leads into the Plymouth and Tavistock highway, just before reaching which, and not far from Roborough village, we shall notice an object in the bank, on our left, which will detain us for a brief space. It has the appearance of a socket stone of a cross and may indeed be such. It is about three feet square, but in place of the ordinary socket of a few inches deep, the centre is pierced entirely through. This of itself, though certainly unusual, would not be a sufficient reason for questioning its character, but there are other circumstances that afford some grounds for doing so.

As we shall shortly see, there are two other stones a few miles distant, precisely similar, and situated, if not so near as is this, yet not very far from the old disused Dartmoor tramway, and it has occurred to me that they may have been brought by means of it to the localities where we now see them, and instead of being socket-stones of crosses, may be something much more modern and prosaic. That a number of large stones were on one occasion brought on the waggons and unloaded at this very spot, we are old enough to remember. It was for the purpose of throwing a barricade across the road, then recently constructed, and relative to which there was a dispute.

Against this we have to set the fact that not only is this stone, and the two others alluded to, situated just where we should expect to find a cross, but also that there does exist an undoubted example of the socket-stone of a Dartmoor cross being pierced through. This will come under our notice in a succeeding chapter, and when we have seen all these stones we may perhaps think that after all we shall be right in regarding them as bases that once supported crosses. We shall then have excellent grounds for believing that we can fix the approximate site of another of the boundary marks mentioned in the deed of Amicia; that we see, in fact, in this stone near Roborough the base of the ancient Copriscrosse.

That it stood on this road is certain. The boundary of the manor, or parish, as we have said is conterminous with it, and the words of the deed are also clear, for it describes it as running from Woolwell "per viam quæ ducit de Sutton ad Tavistock ad Copriscrosse."

By this road we shall now make our way to Roborough Down, and shortly after passing the entrance to Maristowe shall turn into the Buckland road on the left. Noticing the grounds of Bickham as we proceed, we soon reach one of the entrances to the abbey demesne, near which we can look down upon the buildings that now stand on the site of that religious house for the support of which the Lady Amicia freely gave so much wealth. Little remains of the original structure, for not many years after the dissolution the abbey was converted into a residence by Sir Richard Grenville. In 1580 he sold it to John Hele and Christopher Harris, and in the following year it was disposed of by them to Sir Francis Drake, and it is now the property of a descendant.

Sir Francis kept prisoner at Buckland Abbey one of the vice-admirals of the Armada, Don Pedro de Valdez, until the ransom that he had demanded was forthcoming. Here are portraits of this Spaniard, and also of Charles II. and his consort, and Nell Gwynne, as well as one of Sir Francis himself.

The village of Buckland is about a mile distant from the abbey, and is pleasingly situated on a slope that descends to the Tavy. Many of the houses have an old-time air about them, and being removed some distance from a high-road the place wears a look of repose. Here, just within the churchyard, is a remarkably fine modern cross, set upon the ancient base. It was erected in 1898 as a memorial of the Diamond Jubilee of Her late Majesty, and forms a striking feature in the place.

It formerly stood on the opposite side of the road, and during later years the open space on which it was originally erected was partly built on, one end of a row of cottages being quite close to the dilapidated pedestal. In 1892 an old man, who was then seventy-three years of age, told me that he remembered when the space around the base was clear, and that when a lad he assisted the mason in the building of the cottages. He did not, however, recollect having seen the cross in its place on the pedestal. All that remained at the date above named was a confused heap of large stones, that had formed the pedestal, but whether this consisted of three or four stages, could not then be very well determined. It was surmounted by the socket-stone, which, however, was displaced. This was a very fine block, and like the pedestal was octagonal in shape.

The new shaft, which is of considerable height, is formed of three pieces of granite, on which is a beautiful lantern cross, and the restoration which was carried out by Mr. Sedding, has been most carefully done, and with a due regard to the retention of all the old stones as far as was possible. An examination of the stones showed that there were originally four stages forming the base. To complete this, twelve new stones were required, but some are only small ones. These are of granite, but the old ones are of Roborough Down stone.

What was considered to have been a portion of the original shaft stands in the churchyard, near the gate, and has a sundial fixed upon it. Excavation, however, proved that this column could never have belonged to the shaft, as the part beneath the surface was found to be in a rough state. It is therefore probable that it was made for the purpose which it now serves. The pillar is about four feet in height, and is surmounted by an ancient sculptured capital, which being of the same kind of stone as the original base of the cross may not improbably have formed a cap to its shaft.

Two stones, which appear to be parts of a cross, are to be found at Milton, a hamlet in the parish, and these were examined when the restoration had been decided upon in the hope that they might prove to be fragments of the old Buckland Cross. But their character did not show that this was likely, and it was therefore decided to erect an entirely new shaft.

The lantern exhibits some very fine carving. There are figures of St. Bernard, St. Andrew, to whom the church is dedicated, the arms of the See of Exeter, and of Buckland Abbey. A small Latin cross surmounts the whole.

There being scarcely sufficient space in the village street for the cross, a site was found for it in the churchyard. It stands on the spot occupied for many years by a noble horse-chestnut tree, that was destroyed by the blizzard of 1891.

At the inauguration there was a short service in the church, and addresses were delivered from the steps of the cross.

There is a school close at hand, founded by Lady Modyford in 1702, and, as a tablet states, repaired by Sir Masseh Lopes in 1830. Over the porch is a small granite cross.

Two inscribed stones have been found at Buckland, and are noticed in a succeeding chapter.

Shortly after leaving the village on our way to Roborough Down, and just before reaching the entrance to the vicarage, in a gateway of a field belonging to Crapstone Farm, may be seen what has been thought to be the upper portion of the Buckland Cross. It now serves the purpose of a gate-post. In shape it is octagonal and stands thirty-nine inches above the ground, tapering very slightly. At the top it is thirty-four inches in girth. Hinges fixed into it, which are not now used, show that it has also been made to serve as a gate-post in some other position.

In the valley on our left as we return over Roborough Down, lies the large village of Horrabridge. Built into the northern parapet of the bridge which there spans the Walkham is a granite stone having an incised cross upon it, over two feet in height, the lines being some three or four inches wide. The stone fills up the whole thickness of the parapet.

On nearing the Rock Hotel a lane will be observed leading from the down on our right. This will conduct us to the village of Meavy, passing through which once more we again reach Marchants Cross, from which object our investigations will now lead us to Sheepstor.

We have stated in a former chapter that there are grounds for believing that Marchants Cross once bore another name. One of the six crosses we have mentioned as marking at certain points the bounds of the lands given to the Abbey of Buckland, is Smalacumbacrosse. Though we cannot identify with absolute certainty the bound mentioned in the deed which immediately precedes it, there are others named in such close connection as to leave no doubt whatever that it must at least have stood in the immediate vicinity of the spot on which Marchants Cross is reared. Not only does the boundary of the parish of Sheepstor come down to this point, but close to it is a little lateral valley still bearing the name of Smallacombe. While therefore we may not deem the evidence conclusive, it certainly appears highly probable that Marchants Cross and Smalacumbacrosse are one and the same.

This supposition will be strengthened if we consider that we can identify the brook that runs into the Mew a short distance from the cross as the Smalacumbalak, or lake, mentioned in the deed. As it flows from the valley bearing that name we can indeed hardly come to any other conclusion.

Leaving for a time this fine old cross (for we shall return to it in order to resume our journey over the monks' road to Sampford Spiney) we continue on our way, and shall soon find that the lane becomes merely a rough track leading over Lynch Down. We may follow it, and so gain the Sheepstor road at the top of the hill, or we may reach the village by leaving the common and taking a path across the fields. The view from the summit of the hill is of the most extensive character, and on a fine, clear day, will not fail to afford the observer a vast amount of delight. On approaching Sheepstor the visitor begins to feel that before him lies an ideal Dartmoor border settlement. There is the grey moor-stone church, with its strong-looking tower with crocketted pinnacles, at the foot of a huge tor, bold in outline, and with confused masses of granite covering the slope from which it rises. Near the gate of the churchyard is the old priest's house, bearing a date carved upon its wall, and next to it the vicarage, built in a corresponding style, thus harmonizing well with all that surrounds it. There, too, are the rough granite walls of the enclosures, and little cultivated patches creeping up to the rocky common, trees growing in the sheltered part of the combe, and a purling brook with its primitive looking bridge. And above all the feeling that one experiences of having reached the limits of the cultivated country—indeed, what is for some distance behind him is only partially reclaimed—and that before him lies a vast moor, over which he may travel for many miles ere meeting with any sign of man's recent occupation.

Not far from the east end of the churchyard, at a point where one lane joins another, is a granite stone in the hedge, which is the broken base of the old Sheepstor Cross. It occupies a similar position to the one we have examined at Shaugh, but is very much hidden by the growth around it. The cross, though missing from this spot, is not lost, but stands in a field at Burrator, some half-mile distant, where it serves the purpose of a rubbing-post for cattle. To reach it we must proceed on the road leading to the Burrator dam, when we shall soon notice the entrance to the house of that name. As the cross now stands in private property it will of course be necessary to obtain permission to visit it. It will be found in a field overlooking the deep vale of the Mew below Yennadon. It has been sadly mutilated, both arms being broken, but is still far from presenting the appearance of an ordinary granite post, inasmuch as on each of its faces there is a cross cut in relief, extending from what is now the foot of the shaft to where the arms sprung from it; the head also is seen to grow wider as it rises from the fractured arms in the manner of a Maltese cross. The cross cut in relief is an interesting feature, such figures when found upon the Dartmoor examples being almost invariably incised, and it will be noticed that it is very similar to the one sculptured on the slab in the wall of the Church at Meavy. The cross now stands four-and-a-half feet only above the ground.

A good view of Yennadon with the rocks overlooking the yalley of the Mew, across which is thrown the fine dam of the Burrator Reservoir, is presented from the field in which it stands, and quite near to us is Burrator Wood, where is a fine cascade on the stream that courses through it. Burrator was at one time the residence of Sir James Brooke, and he died there in 1868. He was born at Bandel, in Bengal, and became Rajah of Sarawak, being succeeded by his nephew. The house is in a secluded situation, and though around it trees are not lacking, yet the many granite boulders by the little stream near it, and in some of the fields, proclaim its proximity to the moor.

We shall, ere resuming our journey, return to Sheepstor church-town. It is not known to whom the church is dedicated, but there seems to be some probabililty that this was St. Leonard. I have learnt from the Rev. C. H. Crook, the present vicar, that a well formerly existed somewhere near, which was called St. Leonard's Well, and is mentioned in a record of the time of Queen Elizabeth.

The care which the vicar has bestowed upon the church and its immediate surroundings is abundantly evident. Over the south porch are the curious remains of a sun-dial. It is a carving representing a skull wearing a cap rising to a point, resting upon an hour-glass with wings. From the mouth bones are projecting, and ears of corn sprout from the eye-sockets. On a small scroll at the top are the words *Anima resurgat* and lower down *Et sic hora vitæ*; while beneath are the initials J. E. and the date 1640, with the words *Mors janua vitæ* at the bottom.* This very interesting "sermon in stone"

---

* The initials are doubtless those of John Elford, that family having resided in the parish from the end of the fifteenth century until 1748.

is now thoughtfully protected from the action of the weather by a sheet of glass.

At the head of some steps leading from the churchyard to the " Play-field " there is a stile, and one of the posts forming this has been thought to be a portion of a cross. Nothing, however, seems to be known of it.

The old church-house, which immediately adjoins the churchyard, has been converted into a commodious parish-room. This was most carefully done, and with a due regard to the retention, as far as was possible, of the older parts of the building. Close to the church-house, and sheltered by a fine row of trees, is the old bull-ring where the sports of the villagers were held. Its bank is perpendicular and faced with stones, and from the top the villagers could enjoy the " sport," knowing that whatever else the infuriated animal might do, he could not come at them.

In the churchyard is the tomb of Rajah Brooke, of polished red Aberdeen granite.

Sheepstor was until 1877 a chapelry attached to Bickleigh, and in the deed of Amicia is mentioned as such. Its ancient name was Schitestor, or Scitestor.

The tor that overlooks this tiny moorland settlement is of grand proportions, and forms a conspicuous object from any elevated point for many miles round. On the side nearest the church-town is the celebrated Pixies' Cave, which it is said one of the Elfords of Longstone made his place of retreat, when hiding from the followers of Cromwell. Longstone, which afterwards became a farmhouse, is not very far distant. But its surroundings are not as of yore; since the formation of the Burrator Reservoir the valley upon which it looked for so many generations has been turned into a wide lake.

The branch of the Abbots' Way, or Jobbers' Path, that led to Buckland, passed very near to Sheepstor. It is interesting to note that this ancient track has left its name here, a place upon it, some way to the eastward of Sheepstor Church, being called Jobber. We have already shown how the name lingered in that of the trackway in the vicinity of Princetown.

It will be necessary now that we return to Marchants Cross, and once more take for our guide the road so often traversed by the Augustinians of Plympton. This will bring us near to the site of another of the crosses named in the deed of Amicia, as well as into the Countess' manor of Walkhampton.

CHAPTER VIII.

Meavy to Sampford Spiney.

Yennadon—Socket-stone at Dousland—Walkhampton Church—An Old Church-house—Socket-stone—Huckworthy Bridge—Cross on Huckworthy Common—Sampford Spiney Cross—Whitchurch Down.

We have seen that Marchants Cross not only acted as a guide to those who journeyed over the roads we have traced thus far, but also as a boundary to the lands granted to Buckland Abbey. But besides the former there was another path which it served to mark. There is little doubt that the Abbots' Way from Sheepstor to Buckland passed by this spot, so that the cross would act as an assurance also to the travellers on that track that they had not strayed from their way, and would point them to the ford below.

Once more crossing Marchants Bridge, we shall proceed up the lane over which we passed when on our way to Meavy, but leaving that village on our left shall mount the hill to Yennadon. Here, if we leave the road, and make our way to the higher part of the down, we shall not fail to be delighted with the extensive view obtained from it. Rocky steeps, smiling fields, hills covered with gorse and heather, thickly-wooded glens, and wide stretches of common are spread around; and if we are familiar with the writings of Capern, the Devonshire postman poet, his words may possibly recur to us as we look down upon the lovely valley of the winding Mew.

> "The vales of Devonia!
> What landscapes are seen,
> So fertile in beauty,
> So golden and green!"

Passing on our way we arrive at Dousland,* within a very short distance of which is one of the stones alluded to in the preceding chapter, and which we shall find to be of precisely similar character to the holed stone we have already examined near Roborough. It is in a hedge close to a gateway on the

---

* Previous to the adoption by the Railway Company of this mode of spelling the name it was usually spelt Dowsland. But as I find that in 1818 the letter *u* was used, and not *w*, the present form is probably correct.

left of the road leading to Princetown. In shape it is rectangular, measuring three feet by two-and-a-half feet, and, as in the former example, there is a square hole in the centre. This is fifteen inches by twelve, and thus of suitable size to receive the shaft of a cross. That it is the socket-stone of one is very probable, though we should not care to positively pronounce it to be such.

A cross at or near this spot is certainly what we should expect to find, as it would be difficult to suppose that on a road the direction of which was marked by such objects one would not be placed at such an important point. At Dousland the track from Cornwood and Plympton to Sampford Spiney and Tavistock crossed another which the discovery of several crosses in certain situations on the moor enabled me to trace, and which led from the house founded by Amicia at Buckland to the Abbey of Buckfast by way of Fox Tor and Holne; this we shall notice by and by. Here, too, would run the old path from Plymouth to Moreton, the line of which is followed by the present highway, so that a cross at this spot would mark three important roads. But in addition to these considerations we have the fact that the Yanedonecrosse of the Lady Amicia's deed stood somewhere near here, and if the stone we now see be indeed the base of a cross, it is by no means improbable that it once supported the old bond-mark of more than six hundred years ago.

Our way will now lead us by the lane opposite to the hotel at Dousland to Walkhampton, at which place we shall leave it again for a brief space, in order to examine an object near the church, which is situated on an eminence at some distance from the village. As we ascend the hill we shall probably wonder what could have induced the builders of the sacred edifice to choose such an elevated spot on which to rear it, but we shall certainly not find fault with the magnificent view that it commands. Ere we gain the top of the lane we shall pass through a gate reached by some steps, and a footpath having a neatly made stone hedge on each side will lead us to the churchyard. Close to the steps is a large granite stone, built into the hedge, its face forming two panels, in one of which are the letters T B, and in the other the date 168—, both cut in relief. The stone is broken, and the last figure of the date cannot be read.

Cross on Huckworthy Common.

The church is a true type of our moorland sanctuaries, with a substantially-built tower, round which the wind is for ever whistling. Near the south porch is a stone to the memory of Edmond Herring, a former vicar of the parish who died in 1766. Not very far to the east of the church is the old church-house, overlooking the graveyard, and this is the only habitation near. In the wall is a granite stone bearing the date 1598, and the house has a very ancient appearance. There are several old arched granite doorways, and in the passage is a very curious projecting block of granite, quaintly carved to resemble a human face of colossal proportions.

In a corner of the yard, near the door of the house, is another stone like the one we have seen near Roborough, but of more uneven form. It measures some two-and-a-half feet across by three feet or more, and the socket or hole is nearly square, being twelve inches by thirteen. If the Roborough stone and the one at Dousland were really what there is some evidence for supposing them to be, this stone was certainly the base of a cross also.

Descending to Walkhampton we once more follow the road to Sampford Spiney, crossing the Walkham at Huckworthy Bridge, where is a hamlet, most pleasingly placed. The hill on the further side of the bridge is very steep, but not of great length. Our old path diverges from the modern road ere we reach the top, and following this we shall quickly gain a small piece of common, and keeping along by the hedge on our left shall be led directly to the next one of the crosses that mark the road we have been pursuing from Plympton. It stands on a small mound of turf, on the edge of the little common, at a point where a road diverges to Tavistock. It is six-and-a-half feet high, over a foot in width, and about ten inches in average thickness. The arms are short, measuring only one foot seven inches across, the southerly one having a part of it broken off; they are about five inches in depth. The cross is rudely cut, and of similar character to those usually found on the moor. A fine view of Walkhampton Common is obtainable from it, with the rocks of Inga Tor rising to the eastward. Looking up the lane that leads to Tavistock we see Pu Tor, a prominent pile from many points in this locality, rising above the cultivated country in the foreground.

But our road will conduct us along the verge of the common and through enclosed lands to the secluded border hamlet of Sampford Spiney, the last of the possessions of the Priory of Plympton met with on this road.

Here is a very fine cross standing on the green, near the church, and also in proximity to the entrance to the old manor house. It formerly stood in the hedge near by, but was removed to its present more suitable situation by the late Rev. John Hall Parlby, of Manadon, near Plymouth, the lord of the manor. It is seven feet in height, and of a tapering form, and is fixed into a socket cut in a large stone sunk into the ground. A few inches up the shaft the angles are chamfered, as is the case also with the arms and head. The arms are the same in width as those of the cross we have just examined on Huckworthy Common. There is, however, no resemblance between the two, the latter being plainly fashioned and far more ancient than this cross, which is of sixteenth century type. The girth of the shaft at the bottom where the chamfering begins is two feet ten inches, and this diminishes to two feet three inches immediately under the arms: the head rises nine inches above the arms. The spacious green, with the church embosomed in trees, and the fine old manor house, with its arched doorways of granite, forms a most pleasing picture, and one truly characteristic of of the Dartmoor borders.

It has been supposed that the name of the place is derived from *spinetum*, a thornbrake, and both Westcote and Risdon refer to this. But as it was anciently the possession of the family of Spinet or de Spineto, it is much more likely that Sampford owes its adjunct of Spiney to its lords.

The hamlet is distant about four miles from Tavistock, the road to which town passes over the common under Pu Tor, to the northern end of Plaster Down, where it joins the one we left at the cross on Huckworthy Hill. Soon after, it enters upon Whitchurch Down at Warren's Cross, which is merely a cross-road, and passes over nearly its whole length.

On this common the path of former days no doubt merged into one that we have had occasion to notice more than once, and which, as we shall presently find, crossed this down. We allude to the old Abbots' Way, the course of which across the forest we shall next trace, and for this purpose shall now make our way to quite a different part of the moor.

CHAPTER IX.

The Abbots' Way.

An Ancient Track—Brock Hill Mire—Red Lake Ford—Broad Rock—Plym Steps—Springs of the Plym—Siward's Cross—Its Early Mention—Inscription on the Cross—Bond-mark of the Monks' Moor—Course of the Abbots' Way—The Windypost—Moortown—Cross on Whitchurch Down—Monkeys' Castle—A Broken Wayside Cross—Some Tavistock Worthies.

By far the most important track in the south quarter of the forest was the Abbots' Way, which is still in many places a well-defined path, and of considerable use to horsemen. It enters the moor on its south-eastern side in the neighbourhood of Lambsdown Farm, at the head of the valley of Dean Burn, but cannot be traced with any certainty until it is seen at a ford on Dean Moor,* This is on a small stream that runs from Brock Hill Mire into the Avon, and from this point the old road is perfectly distinct as far as Huntingdon Cross. Here it crossed the Avon, but mining operations have obliterated it; it is not seen again until Buckland Ford is reached. This name we shall have no difficulty in connecting with the abbey to which the ancient path conducted. From the ford it is easily traceable for a considerable distance, and is carried up the hill by the side of a hollow. At the top it is crossed by the disused turf tramway, a quarter of a mile or more below Western Whitaburrow, and from this point we shall follow it across the forest.

We shall first trace it to Red Lake Ford, which we may easily do, as this old track is here very plainly marked. It may have crossed the stream at this fording-place, or lower down; at all events, there are evident traces of a path below it, on the left bank. The road on each side of the ford is certainly well-defined, but this would naturally be the case as it is much used by the moormen in driving their cattle to and from the grazing grounds on Green Hill, where is the best pasturage in the south quarter.

---

* *Vide* page 18.

There is a second ford over Red Lake just where it falls into the Erme, and not very far above Erme Pound, and it seems probable that at this point, or near it, another path joined the Abbots' Way. In our notice of Spurrell's Cross we briefly described the course of a track running from the in-country below the Eastern Beacon for some distance over the moor, and which we said could be traced to a wide hollow known as Stony Bottom. This, which is sometimes called the Blackwood Path, though perhaps used as a way to Erme Pound, it is likely was also traversed at times by travellers making for the Abbots' Way from the neighbourhood of Ugborough, and it would be near the point at which we have now arrived that they would strike it.

After passing Red Lake the monks' track is lost for some distance, but that it ran near the left bank of the Erme is evident, for it is observable in two places a little further on, where it crossed Dry Lake and Dark Lake, tributaries of that river, and in each case the ford is close to where the waters unite. Near Dark Lake is the source of the Erme, and the infant stream can be seen trickling from the mire. The latter, however, seems to be filling up; at all events it has been in a very different state within our own recollection. But though its condition may formerly have been such as to present an obstacle to the traveller, it would appear that a means was found to overcome this. The road stops at the edge of it, but as it is to be seen on the rising ground beyond the mire, it is plain that the monks passed that way by riding through the bed of the little stream, where the bottom is hard, and this still affords the horseman a means of crossing.

Not far to the north-west of Erme Head is Broad Rock, which was an important point on the Abbots' Way, for here the old path divided into two branches, one, and that the most used, leading to Buckland, the other to Tavistock.*

The first is still a good hard track, and descends the hill to the Plym, which it crosses at Plym Steps, and shortly after becoming merged into a more modern road,† passes over the

---

* Broad Rock is a mass of granite about three feet in height, and with rounded sides and a fairly level surface with the letters B B—Broad Rock. The initials stand for Blatchford Boundary, the rock making the limits of that manor.

† This road leads to Eylesbarrow Mine.

common towards Sheepstor, as mentioned in the chapter dealing with the boundary crosses of the Lady Amicia's lands.

The other branch it is difficult to trace with any degree of certainty. It seems to have passed very near to the springs of the Plym, where there is a ford, but the road shown on the recent Ordnance Map, and called the Abbots' Way, is for the most part a comparatively modern track, and it is unlikely that the monks' path took that course. We shall in fact meet with few traces of the old road beyond the ford. The traffic over this branch could never have been great, for unless with a special object the traveller from Buckfast to Tavistock would not be likely to choose this way. He would have found it more convenient to have followed the path from Broad Rock to Marchants Cross and thence to Whitchurch Down.

A short distance to the north-east of the cart track which runs over the hill in front of us, and on the side of the upper Swincombe Valley, a triangular shaped stone, having on it a rudely cut cross in relief, was discovered by Dr. A. B. Prowse in 1900. It may possibly have been removed from the Abbots' Way, but if it once formed the head of the pillar near which it was found, as Dr. Prowse reasonably supposes, it is more probable that it served to mark the track described in the next chapter.

Leaving the Plym we proceed in a direction north-west by north, passing over a ridge, where we shall find fairly good ground, and at the distance of about a mile and a half shall come in sight of an object at the foot of a slope which will cause us to quicken our steps towards it.

This is Siward's Cross, a most interesting relic, and though not quite so high as Marchants Cross, is more massive, and is, in fact, the largest of the old crosses on Dartmoor. It is now more frequently called Nun's Cross, and is about two-and-a-half miles to the southward of Princetown. It is fixed in a socket cut in a block of stone sunk nearly level with the ground. In height it is seven feet four inches, and measures two feet eight inches across the arms. The width is rather greater across the head than lower down, being there one foot eight inches, while immediately below the arms it is but one foot six inches. Across the lower part of the shaft it is narrower still, for at the distance of one foot from the bottom it measures only one foot five inches, and below this it narrows gradually towards the socket in which it is placed. These measurements I took on the eastern side. Its average thickness is fourteen inches. The arms spring from the shaft at a distance of five feet nine inches from the bottom, the largest of them, the southerly one, being eleven inches in depth close to the shaft, and the smaller one only eight inches.

At the distance of three feet eight inches from the bottom the shaft has been broken, but an iron clamp on each side now holds it firmly together, and iron wedges also secure it in the socket. The damage was caused by the cross being overturned, but how this occurred remained for many years unknown. In 1889, however, I gathered the particulars from Mr. W. H. Woodley, of Plymouth, a great lover of the moor, who obtained them two or three years previously from one who was concerned in the overthrow of the cross, and on the 10th September in that year Mr. Woodley again saw his informant, when he confirmed his former story. It appears that when a lad he was out with a companion looking for cattle on the moor, and finding that the cross rocked in its socket, they pushed it over, and the shaft broke in two pieces. This was in 1846, but it was soon after repaired by a stonemason named John Newcombe, and when Rowe wrote—in 1848—it was again erect.

It forms one of the boundary marks of the forest, being mentioned in the Perambulation of 1240, and is figured on the old map of the moor already referred to. Here it is represented as standing on steps, in the same manner as Hobajon's Cross, but there is no trace of anything of the kind now. On the back of the map the perambulation is set forth, and at its foot is the following:—

> "hit is to be noatid that on the one syde of the
> crosse abouesaid their is graven in the stone Crux
> Siwardi, and on the oth. side is graven, Roolande."

In the notes to Carrington's *Dartmoor*, however, it is stated that on the western side the words *Bond bond* are to be seen in Saxon characters, having been conjectured, so that work states, to mean the bond or bound of the land, and on the eastern side, in more modern characters, the word *Syward*, considered to be the name of some prince, duke, or earl of the forest. The writer of the Dartmoor portion of *Murray's Handbook for Devonshire*, ed. 1879, Mr. R. J. King, whose acquaintance with Dartmoor was very extensive, renders the inscription on one side as *Syward*, and on the other as *Bod Bonde*, and says it marked the "bonde" between the royal forest and the monks' moor.

Many years ago I examined these inscriptions with great care, and although they are not easily to be made out, yet on the eastern face, across the arms, I think there is unquestionably the word *Syward* or *Siward*. It is uncertain whether the second letter is a *Y* or an *I*, and the first is not very distinct, but the last four there is not much doubt about. On the western face there is a small incised cross in the centre of the shaft, where it is intersected by the arms, and immediately below this are the letters which have been read as *Bod Bond* and also as *Roolande*, and by Mr. Spence Bate as *Booford*, but which I was the first to decipher. Siward's Cross, is, as we have already observed, named in the deed of Amicia as one of the boundary marks of her lands, which comprised, among other manors, that of Walkhampton, the village of which name we have already visited. This manor abuts on the forest, and the boundary line is drawn from Mis Tor to the Plym.* The cross, therefore, in addition to being considered a forest boundary mark, was also a manorial one, and when the lands of the Countess were bestowed upon the monks, it became one to the possessions of Buckland Abbey. It was this fact that enabled me to read the inscription it bears, and to convince me that the letters on it which have been so variously interpreted simply represent the word Boclond. This opinion I find is shared by all writers who have since had occasion to notice the cross. The name, as already stated, is engraved on its western face—the side on which the monk's possessions lay.

---

* "From Walkhampton to the boundaries of Dartmoor, on the northern part of Mistor, and thence towards the south by the boundaries of the Verderers (regardorum) of Dartmoor, that is to say, by Mistorhead (Mistor panna), and by Hysfochres, and by Siwards Cross and Gyllesburgh and Plymcrundla to the Plym." Deed of Amicia, Countess of Devon. Dr. Oliver's *Monasticon*, p. 383; Mr. J. Brooking Rowe's *Cistercian Houses of Devon, Trans. Devon Assoc.*, vol vii. p. 355. It would seem as though an endeavour was afterwards made to extend these bounds, for one of the abbots was, in 1478, found guilty by a jury at Lydford of intruding upon the prince's land in Dartmoor.

The word is divided, the first three letters forming one line, and the remaining four another, directly under it thus:

BOC
LOND

and this has caused some to imagine that there were two words. How the second syllable should have been read as *Bond*, I cannot conceive, for the **L** is plainly to be discerned. The other letters require a careful examination to determine what they are, but with a very close scrutiny the only one there will be found to be any doubt about is the third, which looks more like an **O** than anything else. This is, however, easily to be accounted for, as the wearing away of a very small portion of the stone would produce this appearance. It is this which has deceived those who have endeavoured to decipher the inscription, and together with the error of reading the first letter as an **R** instead of a **B** (another mistake which might easily occur) has led to the belief that the letters represented the word *Roolande*, but no one has ever suggested any reason why such a name should appear on the cross. Seven letters only can be seen: there does not appear to have been any final **E**.

While, however, we can quite understand such a mistake as the foregoing happening at a period long subsequent to the letters being engraved, it is puzzling to see how it could have arisen at a time when they would not only be plainly decipherable, but the meaning of them also be perfectly understood, as must have been the case if the date of the map is to be referred to the thirteenth century. But this circumstance prohibits our entertaining such a belief, unless the writing on the back can be shown to be of much later date than the map itself, for it is not possible that such an error as that of reading the name as *Roolande* could have arisen until long after the time when it was first engraved on the cross. It therefore appears that the map cannot boast of so great an antiquity as has been supposed; but it may be a copy of an older map, in which case the description of the cross and the drawing of the church, must have been added when the copy was made.*

---

* Mr. Stuart A. Moore, in his *Report* to the *Dartmoor Preservation Association*, 1890-1, refers to this map, and says that the handwriting shows it to be of the middle or latter part of the fifteenth century.

The old spelling, or Saxon form, of the name occurs in the deed of Amicia, as we should expect, and also in the charter of her daughter Isabella de Fortibus, granted in 1291. The name was probably derived from the tenure of the lands, *Boc lond* meaning land held by book, or charter. *Boc* is the Anglo-Saxon word for the beech, and received its other signification in consequence of beech boards having been used for writing on by the Teutons. Dyer, however, states that places or streams which bear the name of Buckland derive it from *ock* or *uck*, "water," as many were so named before the tenure of *Boc* land was known.* But in the present instance we shall have little difficulty in deciding which is the most probable etymology.

The letters on the cross which compose the name of Syward, have been considered to be much more modern than those which we have just been examining, and certainly have that appearance. They were therefore probably cut on the stone long after the cross first obtained that name, in order to perpetuate it.

As this cross was in existence before Buckland Abbey was founded, we know at once that the monks of that house were not the erectors of it; with regard to the monks of Tavistock Abbey, the case is somewhat different. Siward's Cross, standing as it does on the line of the Abbots' Way, would seem, not improbably, to have been set up by the monks of Tavistock, as a mark to point out the direction of this track across the moor. But it has been supposed to have obtained its name from Siward, Earl of Northumberland, who held property near this part of the moor in the Confessor's reign. His possessions, the manors of Tavy and Warne, were certainly a few miles distant from the cross, but as there is reason for believing that the forest was sometimes under grant to a subject in early days, there is nothing improbable in the supposition that it may have been temporarily conferred upon the great Dane, and that the cross was one of his bond-marks. But it may have been erected by the monks of Tavistock nevertheless, for Tavistock Abbey was founded in the tenth century. This, however, is a point which, from the slender evidence we have, it is impossible to determine. Mr. Spence Bate is of opinion that it was

---

* *Restoration of the Ancient Modes of Bestowing Names, etc.*, p. 163.

erected on the site of an old kistvaen, which he considers is the cause of its possessing more than one name, that of the old warrior, whose remains reposed in the rude sarcophagus, adhering to the spot after the erection of the Christian symbol. This is, of course, possible, but I am more inclined to see in the word Nun's a corruption of *nans*, which in Cornu-Celtic means a valley, dale or ravine; the cross stands at the head of the valley where rises the Swincombe, a tributary of the West Dart. The name may, however, be of modern origin, and with little to guide us it would be useless to endeavour to determine its derivation. Whatever our conjectures may be as to who erected this cross, or the meaning of the names it bears, we can at least be sure on some points. We know positively that it was standing as early as 1240, was then known as Siward's Cross, and that it formed one of the boundary marks of the forest.*

Being closely surrounded by higher ground, there is no view from the cross except a peep at Fox Tor down the valley. That tor, however, is seen to better advantage from this spot than from any other. The enclosures of a small moor farm are close at hand, the low thatched out-house being built in true Dartmoor style.

We shall again pass the monks' bond-mark, but for the present bid adieu to this interesting old memorial of other times.

TO SIWARD'S CROSS.

Old cross, how many summers bright have flown
  Since first was here up-reared thy sacred form ;
How many winters hast thou stood alone,
  And braved the storm.

Of those who shaped and fashioned thee with care,
  From the rough block that midst the heather lay,
The memory, like smoke upon the air,
  Has passed away.

At morn, when gladdened by the sun's bright ray,
  The lark poured forth her mountain melody,
Oft has the abbot, passing on his way,
  Gazed upon thee.

---

*In the charter of 1204, by which King John purported to disafforest all Devonshire up to the metes and bounds of Dartmoor and Exmoor, those bounds are referred to as being as they "were in the time of King Henry I."

> When dusky night's advance made daylight flee,
>   Or gathering mists the beaten track would hide,
> The lonely traveller, beholding thee,
>   Has found a guide.
>
> Long in the desert may'st thou stand, old cross,
>   And towards thee ne'er be stretched an unkind hand ;
> But with thy coat of lichen grey and moss,
>   Long may'st thou stand !

Though it is not possible to identify any existing path in this part of the moor with the Abbots' Way, the name of Jobbers' Cross occurring in connection with the old track near the Prison at Princetown, as before mentioned, certainly leads to the supposition that it must have passed that way. The course one would more readily imagine that it took would be to the westward of North Hisworthy Tor,* instead of to the eastward of it, the side on which Princetown lies, for in such a case a more direct line to Tavistock from South Hisworthy Tor would have been followed. But the former existence of the old track at Princetown is a strong piece of evidence that this was not the case.

Though we do not know precisely where this branch of the Abbots' Way crossed the Walkham, it seems probable that it was not far below the present Merivale Bridge. Thither we shall now proceed, and on the further side of the river shall pass near Vixen Tor, and leaving the road on our right shall cross Beckamoor Combe to Feather Tor, which is situated a little to the northward of Pu Tor.

Here conspicuously placed is a cross, and on nearing it we shall find it to be a remarkably fine example. It is known in the vicinity as the Windypost or Windystone, but is sometimes called Beckamoor Cross. It stands on an elevated plain between Feather Tor and Barn Hill, being close to the former, which is a tor of small size. The shaft and arms are octagonal ; the former are three feet four inches in girth, and the latter a little less. It is seven feet in height, and across the arms measures two feet three inches ; the distance of the under surface of the arms from the bottom of the shaft is five feet. The faces of this cross look nearly due north and south, and it inclines out of the perpendicular ; a straight line

---

*Commonly called North Hessary Tor. South Hisworthy Tor is now generally known in the vicinity as Look-out Tor.

drawn from the under surface of the arm, close to the shaft on the western side, would fall seven inches off from the bottom. The broad arrow has been cut on it, I presume, by the Ordnance surveyors.

Some moss and lichen are seen on the head of this interesting relic, telling us of its age, like the silvered hair of an old man. Time, however, has dealt gently with it, for it is in a very good state of preservation, and shows but few signs of the winter storms to which it has for long years been exposed.

From its style this cross would appear to be of sixteenth century erection, and it could not therefore have marked the Abbots' Way. But as the branch of that path which led to Tavistock must have passed very near to its site, it is not altogether unlikely that it replaced an older stone. It is pointed out by the moormen that the Windypost stands in a direct line between a fine menhir, connected with the stone rows on Long Ash Hill, near Merivale Bridge, towards the east, and a cross on Whitchurch Down, to be presently noticed, towards the west. That a more recent path than that of the monks passed this way, we shall see in a succeeding chapter, and that the three objects mentioned marked its course there is little doubt. As this must also have been the general direction of the Abbots' Way, there seems to be good reason for supposing that the more modern track here followed the line of the ancient one.

From the Windypost the path will lead us down the hill towards Moortown, where we pass over ground doubtless often traversed by the monks.

"Moretown," says Risdon, "hath long been in the tenure of Moringe, a family which anciently wrote themselves De la More, which place bordereth on the skirts of the moor." Some lofty trees grow round the house, and a pleasant lane near it leads from the moor, presenting a striking contrast to the wild heath we have just left, thickly strewn with its scattered granite boulders. On nearing the end of the lane an ascent is before us, and up this we make our way, to shortly find ourselves on Whitchurch Down. We pursue a straight course, and soon an object is revealed which will become a guide to us, as it has been to others in the long-past years.

Cross on Whitchurch Down.

> "Hard by the wayside I found a cross,
>   That made me breathe a pray'r upon the spot.—
> * * * * * * *
> Methought, the claims of Charity to urge
> More forcibly, along with Faith and Hope,
> The pious choice had pitch'd upon the verge
>   Of a delicious slope,
> Giving the eye much variegated scope;—
> 'Look round,' it whisper'd, 'on that prospect rare,
> Those vales so verdant, and those hills so blue;
> Enjoy the sunny world, so fresh, and fair.' "*

The cross stands near the centre of the down, and not far from the highway leading to Tavistock. It has a very rugged appearance, and the depth of the arms, which are roughly shapen, will at once strike the observer as being much greater than is generally the case, this being no less than eighteen inches. The shaft measures four feet eight inches from the bottom to the under surface of the arms; its full height being seven feet nine inches. In width it is about twelve or thirteen inches, and in thickness varies from ten to twelve. The arms are two feet four inches across. This venerable cross leans slightly on one side, and its rude fashioning presents a great contrast to the care displayed in the shaping of the Windypost.

On the south-east face there is something which bears a faint resemblance to an incised cross, but the granite is so much worn by the weather that it is impossible to determine with any degree of certainty whether the marks are artificial or not.

It will be noticed that the cross stands within a circular enclosure formed by a low bank of turf, which includes a small quarry in its area. This enclosure is four hundred and seventy feet in circumference, the measurement being taken on the top of the bank, which is much overgrown with heather in places.

On the further side of the road, and on the verge of the down, is a piece of wall having the appearance of the remains of some building. The site is known as Monkeys' Castle, which is probably a corruption of *monks*, and may point to some connection with the brothers of the abbey.

---

* Hood, *Ode to Rae Wilson.*

Though standing on the line of the Abbots' Way, the appearance of this cross would seem to warrant the supposition that it is of earlier date than either of the religious houses of the moorland borders.

It used to be related in the neighbourhood that refractory prisoners of war were brought to this weather-beaten stone from Princetown to be whipped, but what gave rise to such a report it is not easy to see.

At this part of the down the track we have been lately noticing was joined by the one which we have already followed from Plympton through Sampford Spiney, for though all traces of these ancient paths have disappeared, it is certain that from near this cross to the town of Tavistock they were one. We take the road leading to that place, but before quitting the down shall find yet another cross. On nearing the northern end of the common, where the road descends to Vigo Bridge, it will be seen close to the wayside. Like so many other examples, it has been sadly mutilated, the head and arms, with the socket-stone, alone remaining.

It is this cross to which we have referred as having the hole for the reception of the shaft cut entirely through the base, in the manner seen in the stones we have already examined at Roborough, and at Dousland and Walkhampton. As this is an undoubted base of a cross, and yet similar to the stones named, we may perhaps consider that we have now a very strong reason for regarding them as having been designed for a like purpose.

The stone is sunk into the ground, its surface being level with the turf, and is in two parts, having by some means been broken completely across. The socket is square, but has the corners rounded, and in this the head is fixed. Of the shaft below the arms, which are a little over two feet across, and project about seven inches, only some three or four inches remain; above them the head rises thirteen inches. In the centre where the shaft is intersected by the arms there is a small incised cross.

This is the last of the interesting objects we have here attempted to describe, that we shall meet with on the path leading to the great Benedictine foundation on the banks of the Tavy. Among those crosses that we have seen marking the direction of the various roads by which it was approached, there are some that were evidently primarily erected for that purpose. Of these we are able to approximate the date, since it is likely that they would be set up at an early period in the history of the religious houses. Tavistock Abbey was founded in 961, and Plympton Priory before the middle of the thirteenth century; Buckfast, enlarged in 1137, was founded before the Conquest, while the date of Buckland, as we have seen, was 1278. It therefore appears certain that most of the crosses on these monks' paths date back to the twelfth century, while some may be even older than that.

And now as we make our way towards the ancient town which for so long has been our goal, thoughts of other days will perhaps crowd into our mind. We shall think of the time when the rich abbey, commenced by Ordgar and finished by his son Ordulph, flourished there; of the Saxon School, and of the printing press, and the monk Dan Thomas Rychard, who in 1525 "emprented in the exempt Monastery of Tavestok in Denshyre" a translation of Boetius *De Consolatione Philosophiæ*. We shall think too of Francis Drake, that brave " sea-dog " of Devon, who first drew breath beside fair Tavy's stream; of Browne, the author of *Britannia's Pastorals* and of the well-known lines on *Lydford Law*, and the recollection of the fare he obtained on his visit to that place—the "tythen pig" between "nine good stomachs," and the "glass of drink" ("claret *when it was in France*")—will bring a smile to our faces; and as some of the beautiful descriptions of sylvan scenery in the *Pastorals* recur to us, and the story of the loves of the Walla and the Tavy is brought to our mind, we shall see in imagination the "all joysome grove," the bowers, and the "shading trees" of which he sings, and hear the feathered melodists of the woods mingling their carols with the loud murmuring of the "voiceful stream."

> " So numberless the songsters are that sing
> In the sweet groves of the too careless spring,
> That I no sooner could the hearing lose
> Of one of them, but straight another rose,
> And perching deftly on a quaking spray,
> Nigh tir'd herself to make her hearer stay."*

**Britannia's Pastorals.* Book ii., Song 3.

CHAPTER X.

A Green Path of the Moor.

Buckland to the South-east Border—Crazy Well Pool—Piers Gaveston—A Broken Cross—Remains of Cross by the Wayside—Stone Pillar—Fox Tor—Tomb of Childe the Hunter—A Tradition of the Forest—A Despoiled Monument—Discovery of a Kistvaen—Death of the Lord of Plymstock—Fox Tor Newtake and its Crosses—Crosses on Ter Hill—Stannaburrows—The Down Ridge Crosses—Horse Ford—Horn's Cross—An Old Road—Queen Victoria's Cross at Hexworthy—Holne Moor—Cross in Holne Churchyard—Birthplace of Charles Kingsley—Cross at Hawson—Buckfast Abbey—Base at Ashburton—Cross at Gulwell.

Deferring for a time our notice of certain interesting objects in the town on the Tavy to which our journeyings have brought us, we shall for the present again turn our attention to the south quarter of the forest.

The road from Marchants Cross to Sampford Spiney was crossed at Dousland by another, which, as I have already mentioned, my discovery of several prostrate crosses had revealed to me. Being marked by such a number of these objects, and pointing as it does to Buckland on the western side of the moor and to Buckfast on the south-east, it certainly seems probable that it was used by the monks of those houses, though the Abbots' Way was a much more direct route between them. It would, however, have been necessary to the first-named house if they desired to reach the part of the moor lying to the eastward of Dartmeet, to which a branch of it went, and they may have had occasion to do so. But however this may be, it is plain that a track ran over the forest from Walkhampton Common to Holne Moor, and the common lands of Widecombe. This we shall now endeavour to trace, and shall commence our journey at Dousland.

Proceeding up the Princetown road we diverge across the common on the right, and follow the lane to Lowery, a farm on the verge of the waste. Here the scenery is of a remarkably romantic character, and is not surpassed in any part of the borderland of Dartmoor. There is a grand group of tors, their rugged peaks towering high above the partially cultivated combes which here run up into the moor. Sheepstor is the conspicuous feature in the view, and its dimensions are very strikingly presented. Below us is the lake-like expanse of water forming the Burrator Reservoir. On our left as we advance is Lether Tor, which we see to great advantage, and below it the farm which bears its name. Passing this, we cross one of the branches of the Mew at Lether Tor Bridge, the construction of which is similar to that of the older clappers on the moor, and proceeding on our way shall be struck with the fine outline of another tor immediately in front of us. This is Down Tor, and we shall notice that the masses of granite on its summit lie amid patches of turf and heather, its appearance presenting a decided contrast to Lether Tor, which is composed entirely of piles of rock.

Passing a farm called Kingsett on our right, we leave the enclosures and enter on the common, and shall find that our road has now degenerated into a very rough track indeed, suitable only as a bridle-path, or for peat carts. Close to it, on the left is Crazy Well Pool, and it is here, near its brink, that we shall discover the first in the line of crosses stretching over the forest.

A gully will be noticed on the left of the road, with a little brook issuing from it, and crossing our path. This gully we shall not pass, but shall keep along its verge, and shall be led directly to the pool.

Lying in a deep hollow, Crazy Well Pool bursts upon the view suddenly, but the best effect is produced by sighting it first from the northern side, where the bank is highest, and where a few steps will bring to our view—as by the wand of an enchanter—a broad, deep tarn, where, but a moment before, a common covered with gorse and heather, with a few scattered hillocks, alone met the eye.

There is no doubt that this hollow is an artificial excavation, the remains, in all probability, of mining operations, numerous old workings of a similar character being found about this part of the common.

A belief has arisen among the country people that the pool ebbs and flows with the tide, and that it is fathomless, the old story being still related on the moor that the bell-ropes of Walkhampton Church were once tied together, and let down into the pool, without finding any bottom. According to Rowe, however, the pool was drained nearly dry, in the year 1844, in order to supply the deficiencies of the leat near by, and its depth was then ascertained.

There is a ballad, by the Rev. John Johns, son of Mr. A. B. Johns, a Plymouth artist, founded on a tradition that Piers Gaveston was concealed on the moor during one of his banishments, and the scene of it is laid at Crazy Well Pool. Here, at early dawn, clothed in a peasant's dress, Gaveston awaits the coming of the Witch of Sheepstor:

> "'Where lags the witch? she willed me wait
> Beside this mere at daybreak hour,
> When mingling in the distance safe
> The forms of cloud and tor.
>
> 'She comes not yet; 'tis a wild place—
> The turf is dank, the air is cold;
> Sweeter, I ween. on kingly dais,
> To kiss the circling gold;
>
> Sweeter in courtly dance to tell
> Love tales in lovely ears;
> Or hear, high placed in knightly selle,
> The crash of knightly spears.
>
> 'What would they say, who knew me then,
> Teacher of that gay school,
> To see me guest of savage men
> Beside this Dartmoor pool?'"

The witch comes not, but Gaveston sees her face grow out of his own, as he peers into the pool; and letters formed by a rush moving over the surface of the water, enable him to read his fate,

> "*Fear not, thou favourite of a king,
> That humbled head shall soon be high.*"

Alas! A double meaning was contained in those words, as Gaveston learned too late. He returned to court, and once more basked in the sunshine of the royal favour, but a cruel fate at last overtook him:

> " Beside the block his thoughts recall
> That scene of mountain sorcery—
> Too late! for high on Warwick wall
> In one brief hour his head must be."

---

* Johns, *Gaveston on Dartmoor.*

The cross, of which only the head now remains, is lying near the edge of the pool, and probably not far from its original site. It is particularly unfortunate that it should have been overturned and shattered, for no spot could be more fitting for it than the bank of the silent pool.

Regaining the road, near the little stream which flows from below the pool, we continue on our way, and shortly come in sight of a ravine sloping down to the southern branch of the Mew.* When about a half a mile from this ravine, we leave the road a little on our left, and at the distance of a few score yards from it, shall come upon the second of the crosses which compose the line extending from this common to Holne Moor. It is unfortunately broken, and the lower part of the shaft is gone. We cannot but lament that this is so, and deplore the spirit of wanton spoliation that has raised its hand, here in the wilds, to strike this old relic low.

The portion that remains lies on the ground by the side of the socket stone in which it was once fixed, and measures one foot ten and a half inches across the arms, which are eleven inches deep; the shaft, or what is left of it, being two feet four inches in height. It is eight and a half inches wide below the arms, and the same immediately above them, but gradually widens upwards, being nine and a half inches at the top. The stone in which the socket is cut is very nearly square, measuring two feet eight inches by two feet ten inches, and is one foot nine inches in thickness. The socket measures thirteen inches by eleven and a half, and is six inches deep. the stone, which has been carefully shaped, has been moved from its place, the earth around it having been cleared away, and is now in a sloping position.

We find the socket-stones of several crosses on the moor in this condition, and a moorman once told me it was generally considered that they had been moved from their beds by people who thought they might perhaps find under them "a crock of gold." † That treasure seekers have in many instances overthrown these crosses, and displaced the stones in which they were fixed is not at all unlikely.

---

*This branch is known as Newleycombe Lake, and rises on the southern slope of the high ground eastward of Cramber Tor.

† On Dartmoor these stones are called *troughs*, to which, indeed, they bear a great resemblance.

Resuming our walk along the old road in an easterly direction, we shall soon reach the ravine already observed, and here, near its head, our track crosses the Devonport leat at Older Bridge. Beyond the rising ground in front of us, the path will bring us once more very near to Siward's Cross, which, we shall now percieve, not only served as a mark to the northern branch of the Abbots' Way, but also to the path we are pursuing.

The cart-track goes on to the White Works, an abandoned mine, where are several cottages, but we shall leave it on our left, as it is certain the old path did not run in that direction. Passing the cross we make our way down the valley to the eastward, keeping on the slope of the hill which forms its southern side, and shall thus avoid the extensive Fox Tor Mire. It is here we shall find the pillar near which Dr. Prowse discovered the stone bearing the cross in relief, as mentioned in the preceding chapter.

On nearing Fox Tor, a fairly hard tract of ground, free from heather, and which is known to the moormen as Sand Parks, will be seen stretching from its foot towards the bog. Our path lies across this, and when nearly opposite to the tor, and about a quarter of a mile to the northward of it, we shall discover an object which cannot fail to be regarded with interest by all who find an attraction in the legendary lore of Dartmoor.

This is Childe's Tomb, and it is on this spot the hunter of the old tradition is supposed to have perished.

We first meet with the story of Childe in the pages of Risdon, whose *Survey* was completed about 1630, and the tale is still frequently related by the dwellers on the moor.

> "And when the Christmas tale goes round
> By many a peat fireside,
> The children list, and shrink to hear
> How Childe of Plymstoke died!" *

Risdon says, "It is left us by tradition that one Childe, of Plimstoke, a man of fair possessions, having no issue, ordained, by his will, that wheresoever he should happen to be buried, to that church his lands should belong. It so fortuned, that

---

* Carrington. Ballad of *Childe the Hunter*.

Childe's Tomb.

he riding to hunt in the forest of Dartmore, being in pursuit of his game, casually lost his company, and his way likewise. The season then being so cold, and he so benumed therewith, as he was enforced to kill his horse, and embowelled him, to creep into his belly to get heat; which not able to preserve him, was there frozen to death; and so found, was carried by Tavistoke men to be buried in the church of that abbey; which was not so secretly done but the inhabitants of Plimstoke had knowledge thereof; which to prevent, they resorted to defend the carriage of the corpse over the bridge, where, they conceived, necessity compelled them to pass. But they were deceived by a guile; for the Tavistoke men forthwith built a slight bridge, and passed over at another place without resistance, buried the body, and enjoyed the lands; in memory whereof the bridge beareth the name of *Guilebridge* to this day."*

Further on, in his mention of Dartmoor, Risdon speaks of "three remarkable things" existing there, and says "The second is Childe's of Plimstock's tomb . . . . . which is to be seen in the moor, where he was frozen to death, whereon these verses were once to be read:

"They fyrste that fyndes and brings mee to my grave,
The priorie of Plimstoke they shall have!"†

The tomb continued perfect until about the year 1812, when it was nearly destroyed by the workmen of a Mr. Windeatt, who was building a farmhouse near by. In the notes to Carrington's *Dartmoor*, published in 1826, it is said to have consisted of a pedestal formed by three steps. The lower one was composed of four stones, six feet long by twelves inches square, and the upper ones of eight stones more, which, of course, were smaller. On this was an octagonal stone about three feet high, with a cross fixed upon it. The writer of the notes also states that "a socket and groove for the cross, and the cross itself, with its shaft broken, are the only remains of the tomb," and further says that no one recollected any traces of an inscription on it.

There are several versions of the couplet which Risdon says was once engraven on the tomb, but in them no mention

---

* *Survey of Devon,* pp. 198, 199. Edit. 1811.
† *Ibid*, p. 223.

of a priory is made. Instead of this, "lands" are spoken of, an alteration that later writers probably considered necessary, when they saw that the retention of the word "priorie" would cause the story to be looked upon with suspicion, as we have no knowledge of the existence of any Priory of Plimstock. It is, of course, possible that lands in that parish may have been left to Tavistock Abbey in the manner mentioned in the tradition, but if so, it was probably at an early period, for the manor was already in the possession of that house at the time of the Domesday Survey.

Risdon does not give us any hint as to the date of the occurrence, but Prince states that Childe is supposed to have lived in the reign of Edward III., but what reason there was for such a supposition, we do not know.

Although Risdon tells us that Childe was buried at Tavistock, yet he calls this monument on the moor a tomb, and such it undoubtedly was. If, however, we are to believe that Childe found a grave at the abbey, for what purpose was this tomb on Dartmoor constructed? We might imagine that the "luckless hunter" being found frozen to death, was interred on the spot by those who discovered him, in ignorance of who he was; and that afterwards, on his identity becoming known, the monks of Tavistock opened the tomb and seized his body, having first invented the story of his will, in order to obtain possession of his lands, and that they then raised the monument over the grave where he had first been buried. The fact, however, of the stones of the kistvaen having had a certain amount of labour expended on them, seems to preclude the idea of a hasty burial, such as we should imagine would have taken place on the body of a stranger found on the moor.

It is possible that some confusion may have arisen, Childe, there can scarcely be a doubt, being the same as the Saxon Cild, a common and not a proper name. Risdon only relates the story as a tradition, and as there is not the slightest evidence forthcoming in confirmation of it, we can only look upon it as a version of some old legend.

As to the name of Guile Bridge, Mr. A. J. Kemp suggests that by this nothing more is implied than the *Guild* bridge, "particularly as it leads immediately to the guildhall of Tavistock;"* and there is much more probability of the correctness of this derivation, than of the punning origin of the name as recorded by Risdon.

For years the exact site of the tomb of Childe the Hunter was unknown, for the soil having partially covered the scanty remains of it, and filled the stone sarcophagus, there was little by which it might be distinguished. When by dint of careful search I discovered it about twenty years ago, a small mound and some half-buried stones were all that was to be seen. Examination, however, soon convinced me that the lost tomb was found, and that something still remained of that which may certainly be regarded as one of the most interesting among the objects of antiquity on Dartmoor.

The tomb itself I found to be a large kistvaen, of which one of the end-stones and the cover-stone had been removed. It was situated on a little mound, and there were appearances which seemed to indicate that this had been surrounded by a circle of upright stones, such as are often found enclosing kistvaens on the moor. This mound was apparently about fifteen feet in diameter, but it was not possible to take a correct measurement, as it had been nearly destroyed by the despoilers of the tomb. One side and one end of the kistvaen were found to be intact. The side consisted of a large block, five feet six inches long by two feet five inches in depth, and having a thickness of about ten inches. The stone which formed the other side was lying at the bottom of the kist, and was not quite so long as its fellow. The end-stone measured two feet eight inches across, the depth of it being about the same as the large one.

The stones appeared to have been artificially shaped, the kistvaen not being of such rude construction as the examples generally found. On this account it would appear to be of less antiquity, though in plan precisely similar.

Lying near the mound were three stones which had been hewn into shape, and one of them I found to be rudely sculptured. Unfortunately it had been broken, and one portion was missing. It was the base in which the cross was once fixed, the socket sunk in it still remaining in part. There was much more design about it than is shown in the vignette

---

*Notices of Tavistock and its Abbey, p. 17.

in Carrington's *Dartmoor*, which, however, in its main features is, probably, a correct representation of the tomb. The stone measured two feet three inches across. At the distance of thirteen inches from the bottom the corners were chamfered, which gave it an octagonal shape, and five inches higher the sides were sloped. This was continued to the top of the stone, the slope measuring five inches.

One side of the socket, measuring eleven inches, was entire, the greater part of another, measuring nine inches, and a small portion of a third. Its depth was five inches.

Not far from this stone I found another, with smoothed surfaces, three feet seven inches in length, and about thirteen inches square. On one side it had not been worked throughout, a portion in the centre about a third of its length being left in a rough state. I consider this stone to be one of those that formed the upper step of the pedestal or calvary, the unworked side being, of course, the inner one. The smoothed ends on that side were rendered necessary in order to ensure its fitting closely against the stones which ran at right angles to it. This stone shows us that the upper stage of the pedestal was about three and a half feet square.

The third stone was discovered at the opposite side of the mound, and was a much smaller one. It had been smoothed and squared, but was only eighteen inches long, and was evidently a fragment.

Such was all that my investigations on the site of the venerable monument brought to light. Early in the nineteenth century it was standing in the solitude of the moor, the storms and buffetings of the hundreds of winters that had passed since first it was reared having left it uninjured. But the spoliator came, and that which time had spared speedily fell beneath his hand. We cannot but feel indignant when we reflect upon the wanton destruction of this ancient sepulchre.

The writer of the notes to Carrington's *Dartmoor* states that some of the stones of the tomb were appropriated for building and doorsteps, but investigations made several years ago lead me to believe that not many of them were taken to the farmhouse. The three stages forming the pedestal were composed, as already stated, of twelve stones, and of these we have seen one lying near the kistvaen. Three others, I was able to learn, did serve the purpose of steps at the farmhouse, though I have never been fortunate enough to discover them; the remaining eight, however, I did find, and they are happily uninjured.

Between the farmhouse (which is now a ruin, having been abandoned for many years) and the tor, a small stream runs down to fall into the Swincombe river just below. Not far from the house a rude bridge spans this stream, composed of stones laid side by side, and there being no central pier, reaching from one bank to the other. These stones are eight in number, and, without doubt, are those which helped to form the pedestal of the tomb of the "Nimrod of the moor."

On making enquiries about the tomb some twenty years ago, Richard Eden, a moorman of the south quarter, whom I had known for a considerable time, and who was born at Fox Tor farmhouse, about 1823, informed me that these stones were always pointed out to him as having belonged to the tomb, and he said he had heard that there were letters on the under side of them.

This, of course, greatly interested me, and I was in hopes that I should find traces of the couplet which Risdon says was once to be seen on the monument.

A careful examination of these stones, which were raised by means of crowbars, satisfied me, certainly, that they once belonged to the tomb, but at the same time convinced me that they had never borne any inscription whatever.

The longest of these stones measured seven feet and a half; two were seven feet, one was six feet ten inches, and another six feet four inches in length, while the other three were about five feet three inches each. The larger ones were about twenty inches in width, but not quite so much in thickness, and the smaller were about fourteen or fifteen inches wide. These stones had all been worked in a manner somewhat similar to the one I have described as lying near the kistvaen.

The result of my investigations was not a little gratifying. That I had recovered nine stones out of the twelve which formed the pedestal on which the sculptered base had rested, there could not be a doubt. From the measurements left us by Carrington, and the vignette, I saw it would be an easy task to reconstruct the tomb, and by bringing the matter to the notice of those interested in the antiquities of the moor, I hoped to see its restoration undertaken.

This, however, has never been accomplished. It was deemed better to allow the various parts of the old monument to lie where they were, a reproach to the Dartmoor antiquary, and to simply mark its site by setting up on a few of the stones thrown over the kistvaen, a new base and a new cross! No regard whatever was paid to the known form of the tomb, and it would have been far better had it been left untouched.

But we will express a hope that the re-erection of Childe's Tomb may yet be undertaken. Three stones, and the repair of the socket-stone, are all that is needed, with the exception of the cross, to render the parts complete.

Where is the cross? It was seen about 1823, and again in 1825. In the former year the Rev. J. P. Jones published his *Observations on the Antiquities in the Neighbourhood of Moretonhampstead*, and in it he states that a gentleman informed him that a cairn three miles south of the prison at Princetown had been pointed out to him as Childe of Plymstock's tomb, and that a cross was lying near the cairn, a great part of which was destroyed. The situation of the tomb is not given quite correctly, but there is no reason to doubt it was that object which Mr. Jones saw. In 1825 it was visited by Carrington, and, as we have already seen, the cross was then lying by the tomb, with its shaft broken. It must, however, have been removed within a few years after, as Eden, the moorman told me that he did not remember seeing anything of the kind there in his childhood. In 1881 I found the head of a cross in a corner of the Fox Tor enclosures, about half-a-mile from the tomb. Though it is obviously impossible to pronounce it to be the one that once surmounted it, it is not altogether unlikely, as we shall see when we come to examine it. If the restoration of the tomb were decided upon, I would again uggest that this fragment be set upon a shaft, and fixed in the ancient socket-stone. It would preserve it, and there would be less need of new work.

Whatever may be the truth of the tale of Childe of Plymstock, it is certain that something above the ordinary attached to this old tomb, or we should not have found such a monument erected over it. There being so few traditions relating to objects of this kind on the moor, its restoration is rendered doubly desirable.

As we stand beside the dismantled tomb, we shall perhaps feel a melancholy pleasure in giving the rein to our imagination, and looking round upon the lonely valley, endeavour to picture it as the "highland hunter" beheld it in the gloom of that winter evening, when the furious storm beat over him, and, exhausted and weary, he halted beneath the tor and felt he would never reach his home—

> For far and wide the highland lay
> One pathless waste of snow;
> He paused!—the angry heaven above,
> The faithless bog below."*

No shelter is at hand, and death stares the bold hunter in the face. But love of life is strong within him; by slaying his horse and creeping within its disembowelled carcase, he may shield himself from the falling snow. He gazes upon the trusty steed, and the hand that clasps his hunting knife falls powerless by his side. He cannot take the life of that noble animal which has so often borne him over the wide moor. With his head bent low before the raging storm he is pressing close to his master's side, as though for protection, and Childe can scarce suppress a tear as he regards him. But the snow is now deep around them, and further hesitation will involve the hunter's death. Turning away his face that he may not meet the animal's eye as he strikes the blow, Childe plunges his blade into the heart of the faithful brute—

> "And on the ensanguined snow that steed
> Soon stretched his noble form:—
> A shelter from the biting blast—
> A bulwark to the storm:—
>
> In vain—for swift the bleak wind piled
> The snow-drift round the corse;
> And Death his victim struck within
> The disembowell'd horse."†

Bidding adieu to this spot, we shall cross the brook which flows down in front of the ruined farmhouse, and mount the hill on the opposite side. A path known to the moormen as Sandy Way runs near here, which, coming up from Fox Tor

---

* Carrington. Ballad of *Childe the Hunter* †*Ibid*

Mire, goes by way of Aune, or Avon, Head to Holne, and is a shorter route to that place than the one we find marked out by the crosses. We leave the farmhouse on our left, and soon reach the eastern corner of the new take, where close beside the hedge we shall find a very perfect cross.

I took the dimensions of it in the summer of 1878, when it was lying on the ground, in an opening in the wall of the enclosure. It is six feet in height, and two feet four inches across the arms. From the upper surface of these to the top of the shaft it measures nine inches. One of the top corners of the shaft is not square, but there is no appearance of a fracture, so that this want of uniformity seems to be owing to the natural shape of the stone. The corners of the shaft on one side are chamfered at a distance of one foot six inches from the bottom. The angles of this cross are not sharply cut, and it has a rather rude appearance. A few yards from it, fixed firmly in the ground with which its upper surface was level, was the stone on which it had been set up, with a socket of sufficient size to receive the shaft, and of a depth of five inches.

On again visiting the spot in 1879, I was greatly pleased at finding this cross erect, but what was my regret when on passing it in May, 1881, I found it was once more prostrate.* For a few years it remained in this ignoble position, but in 1885 it was set up, through the instrumentality of the Dartmoor Preservation Association, and in the good work I was privileged to assist. The shaft was fixed in the socket with cement, and there is no reason to suppose that it will again be displaced.

Siward's Cross bears nearly due west from this cross, and a straight line from one to the other would pass almost close to Childe's Tomb.

On the occasion of my visit to this spot in 1881, I found the opening in the wall of the new-take had been built up, and that the workmen in obtaining stones for the purpose had unearthed the remains of another cross.† This is the one I

---

* This cross was probably overturned by cattle. I know it to have been upset more than once during the times of the forest drifts.

† Fox Tor New take was one of the enclosures taken by Mr. Lamb, who about that time commenced the folding of Scotch sheep on the moor. The wall, or rather hedge, of stone and turf, being rather dilapidated in places, then underwent complete repair.

Cross in Fox Tor Newtake.

suggest may once have surmounted Childe's Tomb. There is nothing improbable in the supposition, as it may very well have been brought to the house, and not being required there, removed with other material for the wall. It consisted only of the top part of the shaft, with one complete arm, and a portion of the other, and it had evidently been buried for some time. It does not appear to have been quite so large as the one just described. From the top of the shaft to the point of fracture it measures one foot nine inches, and from the extremity of the uninjured arm to the end of the remaining portion of the other, it is two feet one inch.

We now ascend the slope in front of us, still pursuing an easterly direction, and shall soon reach a grassy track, not very plainly marked, except for a short distance, but yet discernible in its course through the heather. Ere we have proceeded far we shall come upon a cross lying by the side of the path, the shaft of which has been broken, but is now repaired.

When I was first informed, by one who had spent all his days in the vicinity, of the existence of crosses on this hill, the stone we have reached lay beside another, now standing erect, rather over a hundred yards distant. A few years later, having brought the matter to the notice of the Dartmoor Preservation Association, it was decided, in 1885, to re-erect them and others in the neighbourhood, the one we have just examined in Fox Tor Newtake being among the number. This cross was moved to its present situation merely for the reason that to have erected it where it lay would have meant placing it almost close to its fellow.

Mr. E. Fearnley Tanner, the honorary secretary of the Association, conducted the operations, and under his direction holes were drilled in the sides of the shaft, and the pieces clamped together. A portion being missing, they did not fit closely, and it cannot be said that the work was altogether satisfactory. However, the cross was set upright in a hole in the ground, there being no socket-stone in which to fix it. In consequence of this it is much to be regretted that it did not long remain erect. One of its arms across which was a deep crack was broken off, soon after it was set up, by cattle using it as a rubbing-post. It has remained in its present prostrate position for years, but if a socket-stone two feet or more in height were provided it might yet stand erect without danger of being overthrown.

The shaft, as now repaired, is about five and a half feet long, but, as already observed, a portion of it is missing. It appears to have been of similar size to the cross beside which it was found, the width across the arms, before the fracture, being precisely the same, namely, two feet two inches. Immediately under the arms it is eleven inches wide, and above them narrows a little towards the top.

Directing our steps to the other cross, we shall find it to be a very fine one, and in a complete state, with the exception of a slight injury to the shaft, a small piece having been broken off one of the corners. Its height is six feet six inches, as measured when it lay upon the turf; its breadth across the arms has just been stated. The depth of these is nine inches, and from their upper surface to the top of the shaft the distance is thirteen inches. The width of the shaft is about ten inches, and the thickness of it about two inches less. Before setting it up we slightly deepened the socket, into which we placed cement, and made the stone firm in which it was cut. This is a block three feet three inches long, by two feet five inches wide.

The late Mr. Coaker, of Sherburton, an estate situated on the tongue of land which is peninsulated by the Swincombe river and the West Dart, several years ago removed this cross, and set it up in the courtyard of his farm. But on this becoming known to the Duchy authorities he was obliged to restore it to its original site, and there it lay until its re-erection in 1885 The damage to the shaft, which fortunately is only trifling, was probably done in removing it.

The track, which the line of crosses we are noticing appears to mark, is here very plainly to be discerned. This is however, owing in great measure to this part of the path having been used within the past hundred years. I have learned in the neighbourhood that when the farmhouse near Fox Tor was built, the timber used in its construction was drawn to the site by a yoke of oxen along this route, and that it is this nineteenth century traffic that we see the marks of now. The grass and the heather have, in many places, long since obliterated the traces of the passing to and fro of the early wayfarer, but the crosses which here and there are found prove the existence of the path, and in this present instance we see the old road which they were set up to mark, made use of after the lapse of several centuries.

A fine view of the central parts of the moor is presented from the high ground on which we stand, and which is known in the vicinity as Terrell—probably Ter Hill.* Numerous hills and tors, which, as yet, we have not seen in our rambles, are now revealed, with many other objects of interest. Princetown lies about north-west, and more to the right and nearer, is Prince Hall, with its plantations of fir. Towards the north Bellaford Tor forms a striking object, with Lough Tor not far from it, below which is Dunnabridge Pound, the enclosure to which cattle and ponies are driven when found unclaimed at the time of the forest drifts. Many moor-farms with here and there a clump of firs, and long lines of grey wall, are also seen, for from this spot we look upon the greater number of the forest enclosures. Hameldon, huge and majestic, rises towards the north-east, and nearer and more to the right are Yar Tor, Sharp Tor and Mil Tor, three heights above the left bank of the Dart.

Turning towards the east we shall observe a hollow, which is known as Skir Gut, down which flows a small stream. This is the Wobrook which rising not very far from the source of the Avon, runs in the opposite direction to that river, and after a course of no great length, passes under Saddle Bridge, and empties itself into the West Dart a short distance below the hamlet of Hexworthy.

We shall notice that the stream makes an abrupt turn towards the east, as we descend the eastern side of Ter Hill. Below the bend the rising ground on the left bank is known as Down Ridge, and it is towards this we must now make our way.

On gaining the bottom of the descent, a path will be observed running at right angles to the direction which we

---

*On the moor I have invariably heard this hill called Terrell, but I have adopted a form of spelling which appears to me to be the correct one. Until my first notice of the hill, in 1883, it had never been mentioned by any writer. On the latest Ordnance Map it is marked as I have rendered it—Ter Hill. It may therefore be necessary to explain that not only was a list of Dartmoor place-names submitted to me for revision before being engraved on the map, but that I also added several.

are following, and crossing the Wobrook at a place called Skir Ford, immediately where the stream turns so abruptly. This old path runs from Hexworthy to the springs of the Avon, and is used by the farmers to bring in their peat.

Leaving the stream a little to the right, we shall notice several small heaps of stones, placed at intervals along the slope. These little mounds which are met with in various parts of Dartmoor are called by the moormen *stannaburrows*, which name is probably derived from the same root as the word *stannary*, and they were probably tin bounds set up by the miners. After passing several of these mounds, we shall reach one by the side of which stands a cross.

The upper portion of this cross lay for years on the ground, but in 1883 I asked a farmer who lives at Hexworthy, near by, named Samuel Smith, to set it up on the mound, and this he did. The lower part of the shaft, measuring about three feet in length lay near by partly buried in the soil. Two years later, on the occasion of the re-erecting the crosses on Terhill, we also repaired this one, clamping the two pieces together, and setting it up by the mound. It was afterwards thrown down, as there was no socket in which to secure it, but it is gratifying to know that it is now again standing erect.

The shaft is about six feet high, and the fracture runs obliquely across its middle; it is rather more than one foot in width, but scarcely eight inches thick. Across the arms the width is two feet five inches, and they are ten inches deep. The head rises about seven or eight inches above them, and is worn a good deal; in fact the cross has altogether a very weather-beaten appearance.

In a direction nearly due east, we shall observe on the brow of the hill on the further side of the Wobrook, a small mound, and within a few score yards of this we shall presently find the remains of another of the interesting abjects of which we are in search. Between it, however, and the cross we have just been examining, and almost in a line with them, is another, directing us to a fording place over the stream. We shall therefore proceed to an inspection of this relic, which is within a few hundred yards of the spot on which we stand.

For many years I was unable to find this cross. I had been informed by a labourer who lived a long time at Hexworthy,

Cross near Skir Ford, Down Ridge.

Cross near Horse Ford, Down Ridge.

that a cross existed not far from the ford, but my searches for it were unattended with success. My informant, although he had never been able to describe the exact spot where he had seen it, and admitted that this had been years before, was yet positive that he was not mistaken. In the summer of 1884 he made a search for it, and with the result that he re-discovered it, and told me of the circumstance. I found that it consisted of the head and arms and a small portion of the shaft, but this being partly covered with turf and heather, its real character was not readily recognizable.

From the top of the shaft to the fracture, which is just below the arms, it measured only two feet; across the arms it was three inches more than this, and they projected seven inches from the shaft. Partly buried in the earth close by was a portion of the broken shaft. This mutilated cross is now fixed in an erect position, on the spot where for so long it remained hidden.

Descending to the stream, which at the foot of Dry Lakes makes another abrupt turn, we shall reach the crossing-place to which the traveller of days gone by was directed by this roughly hewn stone. This is named Horse Ford, and is paved with flat stones, which would seem to indicate that a considerable amount of traffic at one time passed this way. On one of these, on the east side of the ford, is cut a large letter H, denoting the boundary of the parish of Holne, which we have now reached, for on passing over the Wobrook we are no longer in the forest, the stream here forming its limit.

From Horse Ford an ancient road ran down the valley, on the right bank of the Wobrook, and although traces of it are wanting for some little distance, it is plainly to be seen lower down. Below Saddle Bridge it can be traced to the West Dart which it crossed at Week Ford, and again entered the forest, and there it may still be seen running through the enclousures towards the little modern chapel at Huccaby. Thence it went to Dartmeet, where was a clapper, now in part restored, and a ford, and crossing the river entered the parish of Widecombe.

But our purpose does not need that we should follow this road very far. We therefore leave it at Saddle Bridge, where we enter upon the highway from Holne to Princetown, along which we make our way in a north-westerly direction for about three quarters of a mile to Hexworthy, one of the ancient settlements of the forest. Here we find not a cross upon which the storms of hundreds of Dartmoor winters have left their mark, but one of quite recent erection. On the common not far from the Forest Inn, a little wayside hostelry, is Queen Victoria's Cross, set up in October, 1897, to commemorate the Diamond Jubilee of Her late Majesty

It having been decided by the inhabitants of the forest that a cross would be a fitting memorial of the event, a committee was appointed to arrange the details of the matter, and so great was the interest shown, that the desired end was speedily accomplished. The cross, which is of Dartmoor granite, made at the quarries of the Messrs. Duke, at Merivale Bridge, is a very handsome one. It stands on a pedestal of three stages, rising to a height of about four and a half feet. On this is a tapering shaft, surmounted by a head in the form of a Maltese cross, the arms of which are connected by a circlet; the top of this is seven feet ten inches above the pedestal. On the shaft is engraven " V.R., 1837-1897," and the base bears a suitable inscription. A goodly number of people attended the unveiling, at which there was an appropriate service.

Returning to the Wobrook and reaching the mound near Horse Ford, we shall continue to trace the path by which we have crossed the forest, but shall not proceed far ere we perceive the broken cross to which we have already alluded.

It is known as Horn's Cross, and has been very sadly mutilated, nothing but a small portion of the upper part of the shaft, with one complete arm, and what appears to be a piece of the other, now remaining. It is, however, uncertain whether what looks likes an arm may not really be the top of the shaft. This piece is one foot ten inches across, and the other is but one foot four inches. The width of the former is ten inches, and of the latter piece nine inches, the thickness of it being eight inches. A small fragment of stone, probably a portion of the shaft, lies near it.

The socket stone is two feet eleven inches by two feet nine inches, the socket itself measuring one foot two and a half inches, by ten and a half inches, the depth of it being nine inches. From the size of this socket it is evident that the shaft of the cross must have been a great deal wider at the base than at the arms. The stone has been disturbed, being now in a slanting position, and only partly buried in the ground.

Our way is here seen as a distinctly marked path, and is crossed by another, which is now used by the moor farmers in going from the neighbourhood of Hexworthy to Brent. This latter track runs from Cumston or Combestone Tor, to the higher part of the old working connected with Ringleshutts Mine, and crossing Sandy Way goes direct to the Mardle, a little stream which flows by Scoriton. This it crosses at a place called Hapstead Ford, and thence trending along the side of the hill, passes the bottom of a rocky gully known to the moor-men as Snowdon Hole, and so onward by Pupers to Water Oke Corner. Here the Abbots' Way must have passed, although it is not traceable across the turf at this particular spot, but, as already stated, is plainly to be seen at the ford below Brock Hill Mire, a little more than half a mile distant. It is also to be observed in the opposite direction, pointing to a ford at Cross Furzes. The path to Brent goes onward to the enclosed country at Dockwell Gate.

Horn's Cross was probably erected on the spot where we now find it lying in a shattered condition, not only to mark the path across the forest, but to show where the branch diverged to Widecombe, and also where it was crossed by the Brent path.* The track we have followed from Lowery we shall be able to trace to a ford known as Workman's Ford, not far below Ringleshutts Mine, whence it went direct to Holne.

It was the belief of the labourer—William Mann, of Hexworthy—who discovered the cross on Down Ridge near the ford, that there was also a cross somewhere on Holne Moor, but he was not absolutely certain of it. Such may exist in a fallen state, but I have never been able to find it.

---

* Many years ago a farmer of Staddicombe, in Holne parish, used to pasture a flock of sheep with a moorman of the south quarter of the forest, and these were always gathered at Horn's Cross. Here the process of counting, or "telling," was gone through, and from this circumstance the spot came to be known as Stacombe Telling-place. I gathered this about twenty-five years since from a moorman who had lived in the south quarter all his life. It is an instance of how a number of the place-names of Dartmoor have originated.

From Workman's Ford on the Wennaford Brook we shall proceed in a south-easterly direction to the moor gate, and following the road shall soon reach the village of Holne. Here in the churchyard near a fine old yew, will be found a cross, standing on a modern pedestal of three steps. The shaft, which is four feet three inches high, is of a tapering form, and thirty-four inches in girth at the bottom, which lessens to thirty and a half immediately under the arms, and to twenty-seven at the top of the head. Both it and the arms are octagonal in shape; the latter measuring two feet three inches across, and twenty-nine inches in girth. At the corners of the octagon, both on the shaft and arms, there are mouldings, which give this cross an appearance that is not a little striking. The cross stands by a grave, where lies buried a son of the vicar.

Mr. Robert Burnard in his *Dartmoor Pictorial Records* states that the shaft was found acting as a gate-post, and that Mrs. Bridget Lane, who died in 1870, at the age of 92, caused new arms to be set in it, and furnishing it with a pedestal, placed it in the churchyard. So neatly had the arms been fixed that the marks of the fracture are not readily discernible.

In another part of the little churchyard will be found a curious epitaph, and one that has been noticed by several writers. Portions of some of the lines are now obliterated, the slate stone upon which they are graven having become worn. The renderings differ in some slight particulars, but by carefully examining the stone, I have found the following to be a correct version—

> Here lies Poor Old Ned,
> On his last Mattrass bed,
> During life he was honest and free ;
> He knew well the Chace
> But has now run his Race
> And his Name was Collins *D'ye fee.*
> .... Dec. 1780, Aged 77.

In the parish register of burials under the date 1780, is the following entry: "December 29, Edward Collings."

At Holne in 1819, Charles Kingsley was born. His father merely resided there temporarily, afterwards removing to Clovelly, so that only the earliest years of the distinguished writer were spent in this moorland parish. His boyhood was passed on that part of the North Devon coast made so familiar to the readers of *Westward Ho!*

From the village we direct our steps to Play Cross, in which place it is not improbable that we see the original site of the cross now in the churchyard. Descending Langaford Hill we shall proceed by the Buckfastleigh Road towards Hawson, and near the gate leading to the farm shall discover another object of interest. It is the upper portion of a large cross, built into a wall, and was placed there several years since, when the entrance to the farm, close to which it previously stood, was altered. One of the arms was broken off by the wheel of a waggon, but the fragment was fortunately preserved, and is now in its proper position. The cross is some forty or fifty yards from the gate, where I remember seeing it for several years, but it originally stood, I have been told, close to an old oak near the junction of roads hard by. It is now thirty-three inches high, the width of the shaft being nine and a half inches. The depth of the arms is greater than this, being ten and a half inches, and they measure thirty one inches across. The head rises eleven inches above them.

Passing through pleasant lanes, and noticing on our left an eminence, clothed on one side with trees, and on the summit of which is the ancient hill-fort of Hembury Castle, we shall at the distance of about two miles and a half approach the spot where once stood the abbey of Buckfast. The date of its enlargement—1137—has generally been given as that of its foundation, but this was much earlier. We know from Domesday that there was a religious house, having considerable possessions, at a place named Bulfestra, and this place, Mr. J. Brooking Rowe says, there can be no question was Buckfast Abbey.* Within recent years new buildings have been erected upon the site of this ancient house, and again does the monk dwell by the waters of the Dart. A religious community, expelled from France, acquired the site of the abbey, and in 1882, the hymn of praise and the voice of

---

* There is therefore reason for believing the Abbots' Way to be a very ancient track indeed. Siward's Cross, besides being a bond stone, may have marked the path even in the Confessor's time.

supplication was once more heard on that spot from which nearly three centuries and a half before many a poor brother had turned sadly away.

We have reached the end of the green path across the moor. It is silent now, and no one journeys over it, save the herdsman and the upland farmer, or the wanderer seeking, as we have done, to learn something of its character, and to look upon its crumbling waymarks. We have seen the path made by the passing of the abbot's palfrey, and the packhorse of the merchant; we have gazed upon the valley where once uprose Buckfast's Abbey walls, and it needs soon that we return to the banks of the Tavy.

But for a brief space this side of the moor will yet detain us. In the neigbouring town of Ashburton there is that we should see, and thither we now make our way. Proceeding towards Dart Bridge, we pass on our right the hill on which is Buckfastleigh Church, approached from the town, which lies on the other side of it, by a toilsome ascent of a hundred and ninety-five steps. The church possesses a spire, the only one to be seen in the whole of the Dartmoor parishes, and from its elevated situation is a prominent object in the landscape for many miles round. In the churchyard is an old cross, erected over forty years ago by Lady Littler to the memory of one of her family. It had been purchased by Mr. R. J. King, who intended to set it up on Dartmoor, whence it was said to have been brought. But he left the neighbourhood before he was able to carry out his project, and Lady Littler coming to reside at Bigadon, Mr. King's former seat, there found the cross, and used it as a memorial.

A pleasant stroll of some two miles will bring us to Ashburton, an ancient town with many historic associations. In a courtyard in St. Lawrence Lane, a thoroughfare named after the old chantry, the tower of which still stands and now belongs to the Grammar Sehool, may be seen the base of a cross, which has been hollowed out and converted into a trough. It is one foot high, and its shape is octagonal, each of the sides measuring about eighteen inches. There is a plinth, and a moulding round the top, but it is somewhat worn. It has been in its present situation for many years, and was brought, it is said, from Ladwell Orchard, which is not far off. It is, however, supposed that it originally stood by a little spring on the outskirts of the town, called Gulwell, and supported an old cross which we shall now proceed to examine.

A path running behind the houses will take us to the entrance to a field known as Stone Park, across which we make our way to a lane, when we shall observe the spring immediately without the gate. Its water has long been considered of great efficacy in cases of weak eyes, and it has been suggested that its name is a corruption of that of the patron of blind people, Gudula, a Flemish saint, to whom the spring was perhaps dedicated. The Rev. S. Baring-Gould does not, however, incline to this belief, but thinks that we see in the name of the well that of Gulval, a Celtic saint. We shall not find the cross here, but at a farm a little further on, and which bears the same name as the well.

In the lane, and quite close to the wall of the garden in front of the farm house, is a small mounting-block, the top of which is formed by a portion of the interesting object we have come to see. This consists of the shaft only, and if it really was brought from the spring it must have been long ago, for I learnt in 1892 from the late Mr. Perry, the owner of Gulwell, who was then eighty three years of age, that it was in its present situation in the time of his grandfather. The piece of shaft is five feet three inches in length, and for a distance of two feet from the bottom is eleven inches square. Above this it is octagonal, the sides being alternately four and five inches across. The stone is much worn, and would seem, from two holes that are drilled in it, to have been used at some time as a gate-post. The head and arms of this cross are in a building in the farm-court, and upon this portion a large cider vat is resting.

The neighbourhood of Ashburton is full of the picturesque. Our visit to it now has been a brief one, but ere our wanderings are over, we shall look again upon the hills that encircle it.

CHAPTER XI.

From the Tavy to the Taw.

Tavistock—Old Market Cross—Hermitage of St. John—Inscribed Stones—A Period of Religious Activity—Tavistock Abbey—Remains of Cross at Peter Tavy—Steven's Grave—Longtimber Tor—Mary Tavy Clam—Mary Tavy Cross—Forstal Cross—Brent Tor—Lydford—Bra Tor—Base at Sourton—Cross on Sourton Down—An Ancient Inscription—Cross formerly at Okehampton—North Lew Cross—Okehampton Park—Cross at Fitz's Well—Pixy-led Travellers—Inscribed Stones at Belstone and Sticklepath.

There is much of interest to be seen in and around Tavistock, both from a picturesque and an antiquarian point of view, but one object it formerly possessed it now lacks,—vandalism or carelessness has robbed it of its old market-cross.

In relating some matters connected with the town, Mrs. Bray in her *Tamar and Tavy* has a passing reference to it.

"William, the first Duke of Bedford," she says, "built a house for the schoolmaster, and gave him a 'little herb-garden,' rent free. Adjoining the same, and then situated within the churchyard, was the school-house belonging to the town; which John, Earl of Bedford, by his deed poll, dated the 6th of Edw. VI., granted for two hundred years with tolls and profits of three fairs, with a court of pypowder, and a weekly market on Fridays, as benefactions. Since which the town has built at its own cost a market-house, where the cross formerly stood." "All which profits and liberties," continues Mrs. Bray, quoting from a survey and valuation of the site of the abbey of Tavistock, made in 1726, "are within the borough of Tavistock, and for the use of the school-master."* Whether we are to gather from this that the town authorities removed the cross when about to build their market-house, or whether it had been destroyed earlier, is not quite clear, though the former seems the more probable.

---

*Tamar and Tavy (1st. ed.) Vol. III., p. 166.

Mr. A. J. Kempe, the brother of Mrs. Bray, in a paper in the *Gentleman's Magazine*, entitled *Notices of Tavistock and its Abbey*, makes mention of another cross, for in speaking of the hermitage of St. John, which was situated not far from the town, he says, " The holy well is still to be seen with the remains of a cross at its entrance." Mrs Bray does not seem to have been aware of the existence of the latter, for in 1832, two years after the publication of Mr. Kempe's article, she says that no memorial of the hermitage remained with the exception of a spring of the purest kind, while from a passage in Miss Evans' *Home Scenes; or, Tavistock and its Vicinity*, published in 1846, the cross would appear still to have been there. The hermitage was opposite the lower end of the walk by the river under the abbey walls, and in describing this Miss Evans says, " Farther down is another cascade—a natural one, boiling and foaming by, as if scorning the small clear drops that trickle into its heaving bosom from a font, supposed from the remains of a broken cross by its side to have been a holy well, belonging to the hermitage and chapel of St John."* Mrs. Bray refers to an inventory of the treasures of Tavistock Church, preserved among the parish documents, in which mention is made of a hermit having bequeathed to it a silver crucifix, containing a piece of the wood of the true cross, and considers that this was probably the recluse of the cell of St. John

In the vicarage garden, which is adjoining the Bedford Hotel, are three ancient inscribed stones, one of which was found in the town, the other two being those we have alluded to as having been discovered at Buckland Monachorum. They were brought hither and placed in the garden in order to preserve them. Of the existence of the first the Rev. E. A. Bray was informed in 1804 by his father, who in 1780 had caused it to be removed from West Street, where it had formed part of the pavement. This was done in consequence of its having become so slippery as to constitute a danger, and Mr. Bray said he thought he recollected having seen letters on it. This was found to be so, when the Rev. E. A. Bray visited the stone, which had been taken some half mile from the town to form a bridge over a mill leat. He had it

---

*Home Scenes, p. 37.

conveyed to the garden of the abbey house, and on the present vicarage being built for him in 1818, caused it to be taken there and set up where we see it now. The inscription, which is in two lines, reads—NEPRANI FILI CONDEVI (or Conbevi), showing us that the stone was originaly erected to the memory *of Nepranus, son of Condevus* (or Conbevus). Its height is said to be five feet eight inches, and its width one foot eight inches.

Of the stones from Buckland, one was brought to the place it now occupies by Mr. Bray in 1831, and the other by Mr. Hastings Russell, afterwards Duke of Bedford, in 1868. The first of these Mr. Bray found in 1804, serving as a coigne to a blacksmith's shop, near the churchyard at Buckland, having learnt of its existence from Polwhele's *History of Cornwall*. Twenty-seven years later he saw it lying on the ground, the blacksmith's shop having been taken down, and on applying to the lord of the manor, Sir Ralph Lopes, the stone was presented to him, and Mr. Bray removed it to Tavistock on a waggon drawn by three horses. As it stood when set up in his garden its height was a little over seven feet, and its breadth at the bottom seventeen inches and at the top fourteen. The inscription on this stone, also in two lines, is SABIN ⋅ FIL ⋅ MACCODECHET ⋅ , *of Sabinus, son of Maccodechetus*.

The other Buckland stone Mr. Bray found with difficulty, having received no definite information as to its situation. It was serving as a gate-post in a field between Roborough Down and the village, and though Mr. Bray tried to obtain possession of it, he was unable to do so. Its height is less than that of its fellows, being only about four feet. The inscription which it bears is in three lines, and like those on the others, runs lengthwise. It reads—DOBUNN ⋈ FABRIFILI NABARR—*of Dubunnius Faber, son of Nabarrus*, or *Enabarrus*; or it may mean, as Mr. Bray suggests, *of Faber, of the Dobunni, son of Enabarrus*. But what renders this stone particularly interesting is the fact of its not only bearing this inscription in the Roman character, but also in the Ogham, (*ante*. p. 33) so that we have here, as in the case of the Fardle Stone, proof that in this part of the country the symbol of the old Irish language was understood. Indeed, Mr. Brash, author of the learned work on inscriptions in the Ogham character, considers the first name on the stone, and also

Nabarr to be Irish. Mr. R. N. Worth, in his *History of Devon*, says that the inscribed stones of this corner of the county, probably indicate " a period of active mission work on the part of the Irish church, somewhere about the latter part of the fifth and first half of the sixth century."

The abbey of Tavistock, dedicated to S.S. Mary and Rumon, was not completed until 981, twenty years after its foundation, and then had a brief existence of sixteen years only, being burned to the ground by the Danes in 997. But it would appear that it was not long permitted to remain in a ruined condition, for in 1032 we hear of its second abbot, Livingus, being promoted by Canute to the See of Crediton. The last of the abbots, and according to Dr. Oliver, the fortieth, was John Peryn.

On the northern borderland of Dartmoor are several crosses and inscribed stones, and for the purpose of examining these we shall now resume our wanderings. We therefore leave the old town of Tavistock with its historic associations, and make our way by the Okehampton road to Harford Bridge, which we shall cross, and after a pleasant walk, each step drawing us nearer to the moor, shall reach the secluded village of Peter Tavy.

In Miss Evans' *Home Scenes*, than which it would be difficult to find a more charming work descriptive of a rural district, is a notice of Peter Tavy, and a reference to a cross that formerly existed there. From a former sexton who remembered it perfectly well, I learnt several years ago that it stood at a short distance from the churchyard gate. The roadway being narrow, the cross was found to be in the way of the mourners, so the sexton told me, at funerals, and it was consequently taken down, and the stones composing the pedestal thrown on one side. I have not been able to ascertain when this was done, as the sexton could only fix the time by stating that it took place when the school was removed from the building close by, and which is now a cottage. However, it must have been prior to 1846, as Miss Evans' book was published in that year, and when she wrote the cross had disappeared.

On the low wall of the churchyard are laid coping stones of granite, and one of these, on the right of the gate in entering, is wider than its fellows. This stone is none other than the base that once supported the cross, turned upside down. It is nearly square, measuring thirty-three by thirty inches, and is sixteen inches high, and the top edge is bevelled. On the left of the gate, close outside the wall, are five granite stones laid on the ground so as to form a kind of low seat. These stones, I learn, formed part of the pedestal on which the cross stood. They are over a foot square, are all worked stones, and at the end of one there is a tenon. Two of them are about three feet in length, and two are several inches less than this, while the other is about three feet and a half.

A fragment of what is very probably the shaft of this cross is built into a wall near the brook that runs through the village. It was first noticed by the Rev. W. A. G. Gray, the former rector of Meavy.

It is saddening to reflect that this cross should have been so wantonly destroyed. That such objects are permitted to become dilapidated through neglect is a matter for much regret, but it is doubly deplorable when they are swept away by an act of vandalism.

Some worked stones may also be seen in a mounting-block near the cottage door hard by, and opposite this there is one doing duty as a small gate-post, but this has the appearance of a piece of an old mullion.

The quiet of the churchyard at Peter Tavy is wonderfully striking on a summer day, for then the foliage of the noble trees that grow within it, completely embosoming the church, hides all but a bit of blue sky from view, and the visitor feels that he is truly alone with those who sleep beneath the green turf, upon which a patch of sunshine is here and there seen, as the sun darts his rays through some opening in the leafy canopy. Very near the path leading to the south porch are two large tombs side by side, with slabs having letters cut in relief upon them. One is that of Walter Cole, buried in 1663, and the other of Roger Cole buried in 1670, and of his son Walter, who survived him but a year. They have the appearance of one monument, and standing upon massive granite supports, have been likened to a dolmen, or cromlech, though the height is scarcely sufficient to suggest this very forcibly.

The Rev. E. A. Bray in an account of an excursion on the moor, in September, 1802, mentions an upright stone near

Peter Tavy that marked the grave of a suicide. The spot is still known as Stevens' grave, and a small mould of earth is yet distinguishable, but the stone has disappeared. It is situated by the side of a grassy track on the common to the eastward of the village.

The walk from Peter Tavy to Mary Tavy is not a long one, the distance being, as the villagers have it, "one mile from tower to tower." The path will lead us by the river, which here flows through scenery of the most charming description. On a strip of level ground, by the waters of the Tavy, rises Longtimber Tor, a square shaped mass of rock, with perpendicular sides draped with ivy, and embosomed in foliage. It is of considerable size, and when viewed from a distance is strikingly like the ruin of some ancient building. Opposite to this is a dark wall of rock, by which the river sweeps, overhung with trees, that also cover the hill-side above. Further up we shall cross the stream by means of a clam, or narrow wooden bridge, and then ascending a winding path shall enter upon a lane that will bring us immediately to the village.

The churchyard at Mary Tavy was extended in 1880, and the open space upon which the old cross stood included in its boundary, so that this interesting object is now within the gate. It stands upon a pedestal consisting of three stages measuring respectively about nine feet, seven feet, and four feet nine inches square. The lower step is only seven or eight inches high, but the height of the other two is about fourteen or fifteen inches, while the tread of each is rather under one foot. The stone in which the cross is fixed is close upon three feet square, and seventeen inches high, its upper edge being bevelled. Its sides are ornamented with carvings, each being of a different design, the figures bearing some resemblance to mullets and roses in heraldry. The shaft which is of an octagonal form except at its foot, where it is square, is four feet ten inches in height, and upon this is neatly fixed the head and arms, which are modern, the original having by some means been broken off and lost. It is tapering, being thirty-two inches in girth near the bottom, and only twenty-three immediately under the arms.

The stones forming the pedestal are all in their places, and the joints have been cemented, so that the Mary Tavy Cross has certainly been well-cared for. It is rather a pity, however, that the head and arms were not made a little larger; their size is scarcely proportionate to that of the shaft. This new work, in which the octagonal form is preserved, increases the height about fourteen inches, the total from the ground to the top of the cross being ten feet and a half. The arms measure eighteen inches across.

As at Peter Tavy some fine trees grow in the churchyard spreading their boughs over the tombstone that tell us of those who once dwelt in this moorland parish. But the spot has not quite that primitive air belonging to the former, the alterations connected with its extension having robbed it of some of its older features.

Leaving Mary Tavy and entering upon the Tavistock and Okehampton road, we shall make our way to Black Down, at the north-eastern corner of which is a spot known as Fostall cross. Whether a cross ever existed there or not, I have been unable to ascertain. At present a boundary stone stands there, but we might well suppose that in former times a cross was reared near by, as an ancient track known as the Lich Path passed that way.

At the distance of about half-a-mile from the verge of the down we shall leave the highway and strike over the common on the left, in order to visit Lydford. On reaching the higher part of the down we see across the valley to the westward the conical peak of Brent Tor, of which we have had many a distant view during our rambles. On its summit is a little church dedicated, like most ecclesiastical buildings on high places to St. Michael, and traditions, as might natually be expected, are not wanting to account for its erection here. It would have been built at the foot of the tor, we are told, but for the intervention of the arch enemy of mankind, who, it seems as in the case of the church at Plympton St. Mary,* took upon himself to remove the stones which the builders brought to the chosen site to a spot more to his liking. But in this instance he conveyed them to a higher situation instead of to a lower one, possibly in the hope that the trouble of climbing up a steep hill would deter worshippers from attending church

---

*p 43, *ante.*

very frequently. It is also related that the edifice owes its existence to the fulfilment of a vow made by a merchant, who in a dreadful storm at sea, promised St. Michael that if his vessel should reach port in safety he would erect a church, and dedicate it to him, on the first point of land he sighted, and this chanced to be Brent Tor.

It would seem that a cross formerly stood near this hill, for the Rev. E. A. Bray speaks of a stone, which he considered to be the base of one, that lay by the roadside at Brent Tor, when he wrote, in 1802. At an earlier date than that a Michaelmas fair was wont to be held there, he states, and on this stone it was usual during its continuance to erect a pole with a glove, an old custom to which we have already alluded.* In Mr. Bray's time the fair had been removed to Tavistock. The stone has now disappeared, and I can learn nothing whatever of it.

We leave Black Down close to the Lydford railway station, whence a lane will lead us to the village, before reaching which, we pass the celebrated Lydford Gorge, spanned by a single arch, and considered to be one of the curiosities of the county. It is about seventy feet in depth, and very narrow, the sides being of solid rock, and through this dark channel rushes the river Lyd, as it leaves the wild moor country for the wooded valleys of the lowlands.

Lydford, though now but a small village, was in ancient times a borough of importance, and derives a peculiar interest from its long connection with Dartmoor. In its castle, the ruined keep of which is still standing, all such as offended against the forest laws, and the laws of the Stannaries enacted at the Tinners' Parliament held in the centre of the moor, were imprisoned, and judging from the accounts we possess, were very rigorously treated.

There is a stone five feet high, now being used as a gatepost, quite close to the entrance to the churchyard, and this has sometimes been regarded as the shaft of a cross. I am, however, unable to agree with this opinion. The stone shows no sign of having been worked except on one of its faces, and I should be inclined to consider that it had originally formed a sill in some building. Close to it is an old stone bearing

---

*p. 10, *ante*.

the initials of Tavistock and Okehampton, and showing the former town to be distant eight miles and the latter nine.

Near at hand is the Castle Inn, immediately without the door of which, and forming part of the rough pavement, is a stone of a circular shape, having a hole in its centre. This gives it something of the appearance of the socket stone of a cross, but for many years it supported an object of a very different character—the sign-post of the inn. The stone is said to have been made for that purpose, but that it was originally a millstone seems not to be unlikely.

In the churchyard is a massive granite cross, erected over the grave of the wife of Arthur Lock Radford, and near it is another memorial of the dead, of a kind seldom, or never, seen. It is however strikingly appropriate as perpetuating the memory of one who loved the moor. It is simply a large granite boulder with an inscription which tells us that he who rests beneath it is Daniel Radford.

An alternative route from Mary Tavy to Lydford is offered by the main road across Black Down, which may be followed to the Lyd at Skits Bridge, just beyond which a lane leads to the village. By taking this route the visitor will pass a stone by the wayside which is worth a brief notice. It will be seen on the left of the road not long before the bridge is reached, and marks the seventh mile from Tavistock. Whether this was its original purpose it is difficult to say. It is a wide slab about five feet in height, and the sides have been cut away at the top and the bottom, leaving the middle portion projecting in the manner of the arms of a cross. The form is so unusual, the arms projecting only about two inches, and being over two feet in depth, that we should hesitate to pronounce it to be an ancient cross, but rather incline to think that it was fashioned as we now see it at the time it was set up to serve its present purpose. It is, however, equally true that its form is an unusual one for a milestone, and also that it stands in the very situation we should expect to find a cross. It is placed where an old track called the King Way, near the line of which the present highway here runs, diverges from the latter to cross the Lyd at a lower point than the modern bridge. The inscription on its face occupies several lines, and conveys the following information to the traveller: *From Tavistock 7 miles, Okehampton 8, Truro 57.*

Passing through Lydford village, we shall regain the highway close to the Dartmoor Inn, a hostelry well known to the angler and the visitor to this part of the moorland country. We shall not, however, immediately take the road for our guide, as it will first be necessary for us to visit Bra Tor, a striking rock-pile above the left bank of the Lyd. Turning into the lane near the inn a few steps will bring us to the moor-gate, and we shall make our way over High Down towards the river. As we proceed the object which has called us from the road is in full view—a cross standing on the very summit of the tor.

This, which cannot be numbered among Dartmoor's ancient crosses, was erected in 1887 by the late Mr. Widgery, the well-known artist, to commemorate the Jubilee year of Her late Majesty's reign. It is a plain Latin cross, the form most in harmony with the wild surroundings. This, and its position, which is singularly striking, would suffice to show that the hand which set it up was guided by the eye of one who knew how to happily blend the work of art with that of nature.

But while we cannot fail to be pleased with the distant effect we shall find the cross on a near approach to be rather disappointing. It is totally unlike any other on Dartmoor. In place of the fine shaft and head and arms of hewn granite, this cross is built of small roughly cut blocks. No less than eight courses form the shaft; four stones compose the arms, and on these are placed two courses more to represent the head. It is considerably taller than any of the ancient crosses of the moor, being about thirteen feet in height, and is built on the rock, on the very summit of the tor. The cross faces east and west, and on the east side of the base stone of the shaft, which is a little larger than the others, is the following inscription: *W. Widgery, Fecit x Jubilee x V.R.* The letters are cut on the rough surface of the stone.

Returning to the Tavistock and Okehampton highway, or striking across the common and regaining it further on, we shortly pass a roadside inn called the "Fox and Hounds," which is at no great distance from Bridestowe station, and shortly after shall reach the hamlet of Southerleigh. Half-a-mile or so further on we pass through Lake, and still following the road, shall at length arrive at the village of Sourton.

This little settlement lies immediately under the hill on which are the numerous crags known as the Sourton Tors, though between it and that eminence now runs the London and South Western Railway. On the green by the roadside, and not very far from the church, is the base of a cross. It is a roughly worked stone, rectangular in shape, and measuring about three feet across, with a socket nine inches square. The cross itself has disappeared, and nothing seems to be known of it. There were formerly several small granite pillars, exhibiting some rather careful workmanship, lying near this base. They formed the supports to the large granite slabs originally used as gravestones, but which have been employed to pave the churchyard path. These pillars are now built into the wall of the Jubilee Church Room, opened in 1897.

From Sourton the road passes over Prewley Moor, and enters on the enclosed lands again near where a cottage stands, formerly known as Jockey Down's House. A little farther on we reach Sourton Down, now enclosed, and here, close to the hedge on our right, shall perceive a remarkably fine cross. It is rather over eight feet in height, but the arms project barely two-and-a-half inches, and this circumstance, together with the fact of the stone bearing an ancient inscription, has caused some to think it likely that this cross was fashioned out of a primitive menhir.

Mr. C. Spence Bate in a paper in the sixth volume of the *Transactions of the Plymouth Institution* (1866-7), considers this was probably the case, and readers of *John Herring* may possibly remember that the Rev. S. Baring-Gould has also adopted this view.* Immediately under the arms the shaft is fifteen inches wide; the head is rather more than this towards the top, and rises above the arms about nine inches.

The inscription is in three lines, and as in the case of the stones now at Tavistock is cut lengthwise. It is very difficult to make out what it is, but the second word of the first line

---

* "In the midst of Sourton Down stands a very humble tavern, backed by a few stunted trees, twisted and turned from the west; and by the roadside is to be seen a tall granite cross, once a burial monument of a British chief, and bearing an inscription that was cut into and rendered illegible in mediæval times, when the upright stone was converted into a wayside cros." *John Herring*, chap. xxxi. The "humble tavern" has long been closed.

Cross on Sourton Down.

seems to read INCID –. I learn that the Rev. S. Baring-Gould has deciphered this inscription, or part of it, and considers it to be Romano-British. Other letters have been cut upon the stone in more modern times, being the initials of the names of places, the particular face upon which they are incised indicating their direction. Towards the north is the letter H, Hatherleigh; south, T, Tavistock; east, O, Okehampton; and west, L, Launceston.

Our road will be the eastern one, as Okehampton is the next place we shall visit. About eighty paces from this cross stands an old directing-stone, the top of which is mutilated, but there remains sufficient of the inscriptions it once bore to show us that on one side were the words *Hatherleigh Road*, and on the other, *Okehampton Road*. After passing the railway to Holsworthy and North Cornwall, a lane turns on the right, leading to the hamlet of Meldon. There, near a cottage, is an upright slab, which might at first be taken for an ancient stone. It is, however, merely an ingle-stone, left standing when the cottage to which it belonged was demolished.

Just before reaching Okehampton we shall pass the ruins of the castle built by the Norman follower of the Conqueror, Baldwin de Brionys. It rises midst the trees with which the side of the hill is covered, and below it sweeps the West Ockment, a stream that unites with the East Ockment immediately below the town.

There is now no cross at Okehampton, but a reference to one that formerly existed in the town is to be found in a Journal kept by Richard Shebbeare, mayor of the borough in the seventeenth century, and printed in Bridges' *Account of the Barony and Town of Okehampton*.* The entry, the date of which is 26th October, 1696, is as follows :—

> "This day the Lord's Justices' proclamation was proclaymed at the town-hall, at the Crosse and at the markett house . . . . wherein was signified that the King had concluded a peace with the French King, and a bonfire made down at Beare Bridge."

Built into the east wall of Okehampton Church is a stone with an incised cross, and bearing an inscription. It was discovered in the foundations of a former church, and had been used as a building stone. On one side of the incised

---

*Published in parts, about the year 1839. A new edition, with additional chapters, was published in 1889.

cross, near the edge, and running lengthwise, are the words—*Hic Iacet Rober*, and on the other side, similarly placed, *Cub De Mois B.* It has been suggested that the letter B. possibly refers to Brightley, where was formerly a priory. This stood on the bank of the Ockment, about a mile and a half below the town, but there are now few remains of it.

About six miles from Okehampton is North Lew. The parish cannot strictly be regarded as being in the Dartmoor country, but the visitor may well extend his ramble to the village, as there will be found one of the finest among our Devonshire Crosses. For several hundred years the ancient preaching cross, supposed to have been erected by the monks of Tavistock Abbey was a feature in North Lew, but it was at length overthrown and broken. But the base of the cross, standing on three steps, remained, and this has come down to us, grey and weather-worn, it is true, but otherwise uninjured. During recent years the desirability of restoring this venerable monument became recognised, and a movement was at length made. It was carried out under the supervision of Mrs. Worthington, the wife of the rector, the funds necessary for the purpose having been collected by school children, and the unveiling took place on the 20th July, 1900. The Bishop of Bristol officiated at the dedication, and about three hundred persons, grouped around the cross, listened to the address which he delivered.

The pedestal is octagonal in shape, and on the face of the moulded steps some tracery is yet observable. The socket-stone also exhibits similar ornamentation, the whole being far more elaborate than any other ancient base, in, or near, the moor country. The socket itself is twelve inches square, and in this the new cross is now fixed. This is of Dartmoor granite, and is over ten feet in height. At the base it is square, but runs into an elegant tapering octagonal form. It is crowned with an old stone supposed to have been the top of the original shaft. The joints of the stones composing the pedestal have been cemented, and the whole made firm. The restoration of this village cross, to which more than one tradition clings, and which has been so effectively accomplished, will be gratifying to all who love these old memorials, and will lend an additional charm to their visit when their steps shall bring them to North Lew.

From Okehampton we shall make our way up the hill to the park. This is an enclosed portion of the moor and formerly part of the hunting-ground of the old barons. In a return of the boundaries of "the Chase of Okehampton belonging to Henry, Marquis of Exeter," in the 24th of Henry VIII., A.D. 1532-3, two crosses are named as bond marks. The chase seems to have been of considerable size, extending some distance beyond Brightley Bridge on the north. The crosses mentioned in the record are Durdon Cross and Dunsland Cross neither of which were in the district now under notice.

Ere we reach the brow of the hill we shall see close to the corner of an enclosure an old cross set upon a base composed of stones and turf, by the side of a small pool, which is known as Fitz's Well.

It is said that a practice formerly existed among the young persons of the neighbourhood of visiting this well on the morning of Easter Day. It probably had some wonderful powers ascribed to it, and those who gathered round its brink did so, we may suppose, with the idea of discovering their destiny, for which purpose we find springs visited at certain seasons.*

There is another Fitz's Well on Dartmoor, a little to the northward of Princetown, which tradition affirms was erected by Sir John Fitz, in consequence of his having on an occasion of being "pixy-led" on Dartmoor, found that on tasting the water he was able to discover his way home.

A counterpart of this story exists in connection with the well in the park, and was related to me by the late Miss Luxmore, of Okehampton, a lady who found great delight in antiquarian and legendary lore. According to this a man and his wife, who were proceeding from Halstock to Okehampton, by some means lost their way. They tried in vain to find the track leading to the town, and at length the female gave it as her opinion that it was useless for them to continue their search, as it was evident they were under a spell, and consequently all their efforts would be futile. She also asserted that its influence would continue until they discovered

---

* In the journal of Richard Shebbeare is the following entry under date 29th Sep., 1676 : "There was not any water to be seen at Fitze Well, the summer soe hot and dry."

water. After a time they chanced to light upon the well on the brow of the hill above Okehampton, when true to her prophecy, the spell was broken and their way lay plainly before them, with the town they were desirous of reaching lying snugly in the valley below. This experience must have made some impression on their minds, for the man vowed to set up a cross by the well which had been the means of dispelling the uncanny influence by which he had been controlled. He kept his vow, and caused the granite cross that we still see there, to be erected in recognition of his thankfulness at escaping from his perplexities, and as a memorial of the magical effect of the water.

This story is but a variant of the one related of the well on the Blackabrook near Princetown, and the well in Okehampton Park probably bears the same name as the other, in consequence of the park together with the manor of Meldo having once belonged to the family of Fitz.

John Fitz, the old lawyer, erected a small conduit over a spring at his seat of Fitzford, at Tavistock, and Mr. Bray,* referring to this playfully calls him a water-fancier, and states that he had in his possession the old lawyer's autograph (written John Fytz) on the counter-part lease of a field, which gave him liberty to convey water " in pipes of timber, lead, or otherwise," to his house at Fitzford, and which was dated the 10th of Elizabeth. That sovereign began to reign in 1558, and as Mr. Bray points out, the date which is graven on the tablet over the well on the Blackabrook is 1568.

In addition to the date there are also to be seen the letters I.F., and Mr. Bray, in his diary written in 1831, unhesitatingly affirms his belief that John Fitz was the constructor of the edifice over the well.

The moormen often call the spring in Okehampton Park, Spicer's Well, but this is evidently only a corrupted form of "Fice," the name of Fitz being often pronounced in Devonshire, Fize or Fice. They relate that the cross was set up by "a rich gentleman," but for what purpose they are unable to say. In Bridges' *Account of the Barony and Town of Okehampton* it is stated that there existed a tradition which affirmed that the cross was brought to the well from St. Michael's Chapel

---

* *Vide* extract from his Journal, *Borders of the Tamar and the Tavy.* vol. I, p. 301.

of Halstock, vestiges of the foundations of which are to be seen at the eastern end of the park, but I have never heard it so related in the neighbourhood.

Like so many of the Dartmoor examples, the old cross at Fitz's Well is broken, and the lower part of the shaft is not to be found. The portion which remains is very rudely cut, and consists of the upper part of the shaft and the head. The height of this piece is just over three feet, and the breadth across the arms is one foot eight inches, a small piece being broken off one of them. There is an incised cross in the centre of the shaft, where it is intersected by the arms, eight inches by six, and about one and a half inches wide. The thickness of this ancient cross varies, but averages about eight or nine inches; its whole appearance is very rugged.

For a long time the cross lay by the side of the pool. It is now rescued from a position so likely to have brought about its entire destruction, and placed in one not only effective, but in which its preservation is ensured.

From the summit of the hill near Fitz's Well there is a remarkably fine view, the range of country seen towards the north being most varied and extensive. In the valley at our feet lies the town which we have just left, with its church on the hillside at some little distance from it. The remains of the castle of Baldwin de Brionys and the Courtenays with its grey walls clasped by the creeping ivy, are seen amid the trees to the left of the town, and though decayed and crumbling, it is yet lovely in its loneliness, the charm of old age endowing it with an attractiveness which fully compensates it for the loss of its former grandeur.

As we turn our faces moorward we shall be struck with the fine appearance of three tors, at no great distance off, in a south-westerly direction. The furthest of these is Yes Tor, the middle height is West Mil Tor, and the one nearest us, the lowest of the three, is Row Tor; the forest boundary lies on the further side of them, South-eastward are the Belstone tors which look remarkably fine from this spot, backed by the grand old hill of Cosdon.

From Fitz's Well a path leads to Halstock Farm, and this we shall follow, and after passing the homestead shall enter a field known as Chapel Lands, where we may see the low mounds marking the site of the ancient sanctuary above referred to. Crossing this, a path will lead us through the wood down to the East Ockment, where is a ford and stepping-stones, by means of which we gain the opposite bank. Mounting the hill, and keeping a little to our left the while, we shall observe, on reaching the enclosures, a lane leading from the common, and this we shall enter. Soon the gate of the old Belstone rectory will be seen on the right, and we shall pass through it in order to examine a sculptured stone, which we shall find built into a wall not very far from the house. It is a little over four feet in height, and about one foot wide at the bottom, but higher up this increases to over eighteen inches. The lower part of the stone being broken, the device is interfered with there, but a line can be seen running up its centre, for about two-thirds of its length; this is crossed by another, which forms the segment of a circle, near its top, and above this is a circle, within which is a cross. All these markings are incised, the lines being about an inch wide.

I learnt several years ago that this stone was found at the church, in 1861, when some steps leading to the vestry were being taken down, and also that a cross, which was removed from the churchyard, had been built into the wall of a stable near by. But as nothing of the sort can be seen, there is probably some mistake here, the report of the finding of the latter object originating, I suspect, in the discovery of the stone we have just been examining.

A walk of about half a mile will bring us to the village, which we shall find is on the very edge of the moor. There is a green round which the houses cluster, and at one end a diminutive pound, circular in shape. To the east, across the valley of the Taw, rises Cosdon, the hill whence the perambulators of 1240 set out to view the bounds of the royal forest.

From Belstone our ramble will take us to the Okehampton and Exeter road which we shall strike at a little common called Tongue End. Near a smithy a large granite post, now in a slanting position, marks the boundary of the parishes of Belstone and Sampford Courtenay, and about a quarter of a mile from this, on the left of the road as we proceed towards Sticklepath, an inscribed stone will be seen. It stands where Bude Lane diverges from the highway, and is rather over four and a half feet in height, and sixteen inches wide at the

Inscribed Stone, Sticklepath.

bottom, and five or six inches thick. The markings are on three of its sides, the western one being plain. These consist of a circle above a St. Andrew's cross, and other imperfect figures, on the northern side; lines having some faint resemblence to a human form, on the eastern, and on the southern other lines and semi-circles. Mr. Spence Bate has figured this stone in the paper to which we have before referred, and has given a very good representation of the markings.*

Half a mile or so further on the highway runs for a short distance along the verge of the moor, and here, close to the road that comes down from Belstone, and at the entrance to the village of Sticklepath, is another inscribed stone. This is a larger one than that we have just examined, being about five and a half feet in height, and about a foot square, though the sides are not quite of equal size. It bears markings of a similar character, and has in addition a Latin cross cut in relief upon it. It is not easy to say what the rude tracery represents, but there is a figure which may be likened to the outline of the globes of a huge hour glass. There are two St. Andrew's crosses, and the occurrence of this figure on both stones would seem to point to their connection with that saint. The parish church of South Tawton, not a mile distant from this Sticklepath stone, is dedicated to him.

Mr. G. W. Ormerod noticed this stone in a paper read before the members of the Devonshire Association, in 1874;† and he says that it once fell down when a road was cut near it. It has also been mentioned by Mr. C. Spence Bate,‡ and by Mr. Thomas Hughes.§

The stone stands at the entrance of the glen, down which courses the river Taw,

"The long brook falling thro' the clov'n ravine,"

and close beside it is a well, over which is inscribed—

Lady Well. Drink and Be Thankful.

Sticklepath is a pretty little village, and forms a good place whence to commence the ascent of Cosdon. The Dartmoor explorer will also find that from it he can, by making his way up the valley of the Taw, easily gain the recesses of the moor.

---

*Trans. Plymouth Institution, Vol. VI.
†Printed in the sixth volume of the Transactions. The paper is entitled Wayside Crosses in the District Bordering the East of Dartmoor.
‡ Trans. Plymouth Institution, Vol. VI. § Gentleman's Mag., Sept., 1862.

CHAPTER XII.

At the Foot of Cosdon.

Zeal Head Cross—Cross at South Zeal—Story of John Stanbury—Moon's Cross—South Tawton—Oxenham Cross—Tradition of the White Bird—Cross at Ringhole Copse—Cross at Addiscott—Firestone Ley—Cross at West Week—An Ancient Border Farmhouse.

The parish of South Tawton includes within its area the huge hill of Cosdon, the cultivated portion of it lying at the foot of the lofty height, and stretching towards the north-east. Here we shall find no less than six of the interesting objects the examination of which is the purpose of our extended ramble through the moorland region, and shall discover some of them to be more than ordinarily striking.

Leaving Sticklepath we cross the bridge over the Taw, and ascending the hill on the left, shall very soon reach a point where a road to the village of South Tawton branches off. Here a cross, known as Townsend, or Zeal Head Cross, formerly stood, but we shall look in vain for any remains of it now. It was destroyed many years since by one John Orchard, who was afterwards hanged—not for this act of vandalism, but for forgery.

Proceeding down the steep hill before us towards South Zeal, which is now in view, we shall not fail to be struck, on a nearer approach, with its old-fashioned appearance. It consists mainly of one long street, running down this hill and partly up another. Many of the houses are interesting, and the curious observer will find not a little to attract him. But what demands our special attention now is the beautiful cross that the village possesses, and which occupying, as it should do, a prominent situation, will be the very first object on which our eyes will rest as we enter the place. The street is of some width, and in its centre stands the ancient chapel of St. Mary. Extending from this, with the road on each side of it, is a small enclosed piece of ground, planted with shrubs, on which some cottages formerly stood, and at the end of this is the cross. Set up on a very lofty pedestal, the top of this

South Zeal Cross.

cross is at a considerable height from the ground. It rises about nine feet above the base in which it is fixed, while the surface of the latter is about seven feet from the bottom of the pedestal, and two or three feet more from the ground, as the former stands on a foundation of small stones. This pedestal is not formed of large blocks as in the case of those we have examined at Buckland and Meavy, and other places, but the steps composing it, which are three in number, are built of stones of small size with worked granite slabs laid upon them, the edges of which project. The base of the cross is a stone about three feet square, and twenty inches in height, its upper edge being bevelled. The shaft is of an elegant tapering form, one foot square at the bottom, but a short distance from its foot the angles are chamfered, and it becomes octagonal. Just below the arms there is a kind of wide fillet running round it. The head and arms are not one with the shaft, but are fixed upon it. The whole has a very graceful appearance, and with the little chapel of ancient days, forms a most interesting picture, the surroundings harmonizing with it in a truly pleasing manner.

Mr. G. W. Ormerod, in the paper referred to in the previous chapter, and written in 1874, describes this cross, and states that about forty years before that time it was repaired by a stonemason, who was a Roman Catholic, and who made a vow to do so during a storm, when sailing from America to England, should he be permitted to land in safety. His voyage had a happy termination and he performed what he had promised. There are, however, some inaccuracies here, the real facts being, perhaps, scarcely so poetical. There was no storm, and no vow made on board a vessel. About the year 1838, one John Stanbury, who was a native of South Zeal, and a carpenter by trade, came home from America for a short season. Seeing that the cross needed some repair, he effected this himself, and as a memento of his visit to the place of his birth caused his initials and the date to be cut in the base. The villagers, however, objected to the latter part of his work, and destroyed the inscription, the marks of which can still be seen in a small panel on the stone. Taking umbrage at this he made a vow that though circumstances might bring him to England again, he would never more set foot in South Zeal. He returned to America, and twenty-four years afterwards came a second time to his native country. He did not break his vow, for on this occasion South Zeal knew him not, as he remained during his sojourn at Hennock, near Bovey Tracey. John Stanbury, who was a Roman Catholic, died in Brooklyn, New York. These facts were obtained for me from a descendant of his, by Mr. S. Westaway, junr., of South Zeal.

The similarity of the story gathered by Mr. Ormerod to the tradition attaching to Brent Tor, which we have already noticed, renders it more than probable that the former was suggested by the latter.

Close to the chapel of St. Mary a road leads to South Tawton village, which is half-a-mile distant. This we shall follow, and about midway between the two places, or a little beyond, shall reach a large barn, where a road comes in from Zeal Head Cross. In front of this barn is an open space, and here on a bank is the base and part of the shaft of what must have been at one time a large cross. The base, which is ten inches in height, is nearly square, measuring three feet three inches by three feet four, and has the upper corners roughly rounded off. The height of the broken piece of shaft is two feet and a half; it is octagonal in form, and is four feet two inches in girth.

The cross does not stand quite in its original position. This was nearer the centre of the open space, and being in the way it was deemed advisable to set it back a few yards. It is known as Moon's Cross, and marks the spot where the traveller journeying from beyond South Tawton would diverge accordingly as he desired to skirt the northern or eastern edge of Dartmoor.

A pretty rural scene meets our eye in the village of South Tawton, with its open space, in the centre of which is a large tree, and an ancient house with arched doorway near the churchyard gate. The church itself is a fine building, its massive tower being particularly striking, and in the well-kept graveyard many a stone will be seen fashioned from the granite of the moor. We take the road to Oxenham, and passing a mill commence the ascent of a hill. At some distance up the road is crossed by another, leading from South Zeal to North Tawton and Bow. The spot is known as Oxenham Cross, but only a small portion of the shaft, and the mutilated head of the old monument that formerly marked it now remains. This is standing in the hedge, concealed by bushes, on the left in ascending. The piece of shaft was noticed by Mr. G. W. Ormerod in his interesting paper; it is octagonal in shape, and about two feet in height, and three feet seven inches in girth. Mr. Ormerod speaks of it as being between Whiddon Down and Oxenham, but this is not quite correct, as it stands, as now described, on the South Tawton side of Oxenham, whereas Whiddon Down is in the opposite direction.

Some years ago I discovered the upper part of this cross among some stones in a hedge by the side of a gateway near by, though I afterwards learned that its existence was not unknown to two or three in the neighbourhood. This piece is about thirteen inches high and seven inches wide; the top is broken away, and only rises about four inches above the arms. It is one foot across the arms, and where these intersect the shaft there is a small incised Greek cross seven inches high, the lines being an inch and a half wide. The shattered head is now resting on the broken shaft.

Not far from this cross, and in full view from the field in the hedge of which it stands, are many very high mounds of soil thrown out from some quarries which have been worked for a great number of years. They are covered with grass and dotted with trees, and have quite a picturesque appearance.

Passing up the lane the entrance to Oxenham will be observed on the right hand. The ancient mansion no longer exists; the present building is an erection of the last century, and is now used as a farmhouse. With the family of Oxenham is connected a very curious tradition. It is said that a white bird, or one with a white breast, appears as a forewarning of the death of members of the family; that it is "bound" to appear when the head of the family is about to die, and *may* do so just previous to the death of any other of the members. There is an account of its appearance in 1635, which was printed in a tract of twenty pages, in which an allusion occurs to the bird also having appeared in 1618, and several instances have since been recorded, the latest being in 1873.[*]

---

[*]A very exhaustive paper on this curious omen, by Mr. R. W. Cotton, may be seen in the fourteenth volume of *Transactions of the Devonshire Association.*

Continuing the ascent of the hill we shall soon pass a small wood on the left hand. This is Ringhole Copse, and at its higher end a lane leading from the one we saw branching off to North Tawton joins our road. At the junction, and close to the edge of the copse, will be seen an exceedingly fine cross. It is very nearly seven feet and a half in height, and the arms, which are about nine inches deep, measure nineteen inches across; they spring off at about eight or nine inches from the top of the head. The shaft is over a foot wide immediately under the arms, and seven inches thick; between the arms on each face there is incised a small Greek cross. An ash tree spreads its branches over it, the foliage partially concealing its venerable head.

We now retrace our steps, but ere reaching the entrance to Oxenham shall turn down a lane on our left, which will lead us close by the house. We mount a hill, and in a few minutes arrive at the hamlet of Addiscott, where stands a cross which we shall at once perceive to be a beautiful example. It is not of great height, being only four feet eight inches, but it is well-proportioned and care is displayed in its fashioning. The bottom of the shaft, which is set into a worked base, is square, but only preserves this form for a distance of about three inches, where the angles being chamfered, it becomes octagonal, and the arms are also of this shape. In the shaft the faces of the octagon vary in width from four to five inches; in the arms they are each three-and-a-half inches. These latter spring off at a distance of three feet one inch from the surface of the socket-stone, and the head rises eight and a half inches above them. The shaft, which does not taper, is three feet one inch in girth, and the arms, two feet nine and a half inches. The socket-stone, or base, the upper edge of which is sloped, is about nine inches above the ground, and two and a half feet square. This striking cross is not quite in its original position. Mr. George Cann, of Dishcombe, had it placed where it now stands, as it had been decided to remove it from its former site in order that a gateway might be made there. It is pleasing to be able to record an instance of care being taken to preserve a memorial of olden days; had such been more frequent, how much brighter would be the light thrown upon the past.

Cross at Ringhole Copse, South Tawton.

From Addiscott the road ascends to Firestone Ley, a little common, over one side of which runs the Exeter and Okehampton road. This passed through South Zeal, but in the later days of stage coach traffic a new road was made in order to avoid the hills, joining the old one again near the bridge over the Taw at Sticklepath. We shall pass across Firestone Ley, and when at the point where the new road leaves the old one, shall observe on our left a narrow lane. We enter this, and a short distance on shall reach a gate opening upon another lane on the right, a true specimen of a Dartmoor border pathway, and encumbered with blocks of lichen-stained granite. It will conduct us to West Week, an ancient farmhouse of a very interesting character, where just inside the gate, under a tree, is part of what formerly was undoubtedly a fine cross. It now presents the appearance of a Tau cross, as the head is broken completely off, but upon examination the marks of the fracture can be seen. It is fixed upon a mound, roughly faced with stones, thrown up around the trunk of the tree, and is two feet two inches in height. The lower part of the shaft is missing. Its form is octagonal, and it is a little over thirty-seven inches in girth, the arms being an inch or two less. The width across the arms is about thirty-two inches.

It will be seen from the foregoing descriptions that the crosses in the parish of South Tawton are, with the exception of the one at Ringhole Copse, octagonal in shape, and that two of them, namely those at South Zeal and Addiscott, are of more than ordinary beauty.

Opposite to the cross at West Week is a fine old embattled gateway, with a coat of arms carved in granite, telling us something of the former importance of this old moorland dwelling.

CHAPTER XIII.

Throwleigh to Moretonhampstead.

Fragments of Crosses at Throwleigh—An Ancient Base—Restoration of the Cross—Gidleigh—Murchington—Gidleigh Park and Leigh Bridge—Cross at Holy Street—Base of Cross at Chagford—Cross at Way Barton—Surroundings of Chagford—Cross near Cranbrook—Stone Cross—Week Down—Shorter Cross.

The district extending from the village of Throwleigh to Moretonhampstead will now claim our attention, and we shall therefore direct our steps from West Week to the first-named place in order to commence our investigations.

Our way will lead us by some grand old trees, and down a narrow lane, at the bottom of which we pass through a gate by a small farmhouse, and enter upon the Chagford road. Turning southward, with the moor on our right, we shall proceed towards Payne's Bridge, noticing on our way the numerous enclosures which have of late years been made on the skirts of the waste. Crossing the bridge, which spans the Blackaton Brook, a tributary of the Teign, we follow the road over the common, and shortly enter upon the enclosed lands once more. Thence through a pleasant lane we make our way to the small border village.

Here we shall be gratified at observing a recently erected cross, the base, or socket-stone, of which is ancient. It stands on an excellent site at the junction of the South Tawton, Chagford, and Gidleigh roads, and forms a truly interesting feature in the village. The socket-stone, which is nearly square, being thirty-four inches by thirty-two, and thirteen inches high, is placed upon a pedestal of three steps. On this stone, the top corners of which are roughly rounded off, is set the cross, which is about three feet high. The height of the three steps is altogether about two feet; it will thus be seen that the total height of this memorial is six feet. The stages of the pedestal are not quite square, the shape being proportioned to that of the ancient base. The bottom stage measures eight feet nine inches by eight feet six, and the upper one about four feet eleven inches by four feet seven.

The two upper steps bear inscriptions on their fronts, from which we learn that the cross was erected by the rector and a parishioner in the sixtieth year of Queen Victoria. The parishioner is Mrs. Wood, of St. John's, Murchington, and the rector the Rev. George Lincoln Gambier Lowe, to whom not only the dwellers in this moorland parish, but all whose tastes lead them to regard the preservation of our antiquities as a thing to be desired, will feel themselves indebted.

Not many years since the old base, which had been hollowed out to form a shallow trough (this being now filled with cement) was lying neglected near a horse-pond. Mr. Ormerod remembered when the fragments of two crosses, fastened together by an iron spike, stood on this base. One consisted of a portion of an octagonal shaft, two feet seven inches high, and the other of an upper portion of a cross of another pattern, from which one of the arms was missing, but when he saw it in 1872 this piece had been displaced, and was lying in the pond close by.

In 1892 I learnt that these pieces, not being securely fixed, were thrown off by children when at play, and in order that they might not be further mutilated, and with a view to their being afterwards properly set up in their place, they were removed about 1880 by the rector. Nothing more was done, however, and the pieces could not afterwards be found.

The cross originally stood, it is believed, in the churchyard, and fell into a ruinous condition about fifty years ago. Repairs were about that time being carried out, and it is said that the mason built some of the fragments of the cross into a wall.

Throwleigh Church is close at hand, built, like all the border sanctuaries, of the durable granite of the moor. It possesses a remarkably fine priest's doorway.

Our course will next take us along the Chagford road as far as Wonston, whence we may diverge if we please, in order to visit Gidleigh, which is about a mile distant. We shall find there a little church, an old manor house, a diminutive pound, and the ruins of a castle, the latter, however, not being very extensive. The place wears a very primitive air, and for the lover of all that is old-fashioned will certainly possess an attraction. On the adjoining commons, which are soon reached, are several pre-historic monuments of more than ordinary note.

From Wonston we shall cross some path-fields to a little bridge at the foot of a steep hill, then taking the Chagford road we shall ascend towards the hamlet of Murchington. A few years ago, in the garden of St. Olave's, a pleasantly situated residence, then belonging to the Rev. W. T. A. Radford, rector of Down St. Mary, was a fine old cross. It was not a Dartmoor cross, having been brought from the parish of Bow, which is many miles distant. This was done, I have been informed, by the Rev. J. Ingle, a former owner of the property. About three years ago Mr. Radford sold St. Olave's to the Rev. A. G. Barker, and shortly afterwards the rector of Down St. Mary, saying that Mr. Radford had authorized him to remove the cross, took it away, to his own parish, and placed it in the churchyard there, where it now is. There seems, however, to have been a misunderstanding somewhere, as Mr. Barker afterwards ascertained that no permission to remove it had been given. The cross is five feet six inches in height, and nearly two feet across the arms. The corners, with the exception of those at the extremities of the arms and the top of the head, are roughly bevelled.

Shortly before reaching Murchington we turn into the Gidleigh road, from which a lane branches towards the bottom of the valley. Entering this we descend the hill by a narrow pathway on the right to Leigh Steps, by which we shall cross the North Teign. A short distance up the stream is the entrance to Gidleigh Park—or Chase, where is a blending of wildness and sylvan beauty that cannot fail to impress the beholder. But our course leads us to Leigh Bridge, immedialely below which is the confluence of the North and South Teign. The united stream flows onward to Holy Street, where formerly stood the old mill that has formed a subject for so many brushes, since the time it was painted by Creswick. We make our way up the hill, noticing the Puckie—or Pixy—Stone, on our left, below which is Blacksmith's Pool, and very soon afterwards descend towards Holy Street. At a bend in the lane we shall find the upper portion of a cross built into the wall. It is about three feet in height, and the arms measure twenty-seven inches across, one projecting seven inches from the shaft, and the other five. They are not quite of the same depth, being eleven and twelve inches respectively. The width of the shaft immediately under the arms is fourteen inches. In the centre is an incised cross, ten inches high. For the preservation of this old relic we are indebted to the Rev. Arthur Whipham, who placed it where we now see it. It had previously been lying in the yard at Holy Street, and was brought there from Chagford by a Mr. Southmead. It used to stand in, or near, the market-place. and a base of a cross now in the court at the rear of Southmead House, is said to have belonged to it. Mr. Ormerod, however, states that another cross, which will be found at Way Barton, was the one that surmounted this base. That writer, who was for some time resident at Chagford, no doubt had opportunities of ascertaining its history, but I cannot find any other belief now existing than that the base is that of this Holy Street Cross. It is a very handsome example, and while the cross is certainly of simple form, and displays no attempt at ornamentation, the one at Way Barton is of a far ruder type, and it can scarcely be conceived that it ever belonged to such a carefully fashioned socket-stone.

A short walk from Holy Street, past the deserted woollen factory close to the picturesque bridge, will bring us to Chagford, now so well known as a tourist resort. The base of the cross, as we have stated, is at Southmead House, which formerly belonged to the gentleman of that name, and he it was, I have been told, who caused it to be removed here. Seeing that he also took the cross to Holy Street, it would certainly appear probable that the one belonged to the other. The stone has been hollowed out, and now forms a pump trough, but the ornamentation of its sides has not been interfered with. This consists of well-cut mouldings, and gives it an appearance totally different from the other bases we have examined, with the sole exception of the one already noticed at Ashburton.* It is an octagon, measuring forty-four inches across, each of its sides being about nineteen inches.

---

*It is rather singular that these two bases, which are of similar shape, and exhibit much more skill in their fashioning than any others found in the Dartmoor district, should each have been made into water troughs.

It is sunk a little into the ground, and now measures one foot in height; beneath it there is a well.

Way Barton, the residence of Mr. Coniam, is distant not quite a mile from Chagford, on the road to Teigncombe. The old cross to which we have referred is lying at the back of the farm buildings, and, when I first saw it, in 1892, could scarcely be distinguished from a rough gate-post, to which purpose it had, indeed, at some time been put. The position of two or three holes drilled in it to receive the hinges showed that when so used the upper part had been placed in the ground. The head had been knocked off, and apparently the greater portion of the arms also, these being very short, and extremely rough. With the aid of a crowbar, Mr. Coniam's man at my request turned the stone over, and I then discovered an incised Latin cross upon it. The lines of this are very thin, and it was not entire, the top part having been graven on the head of the cross. The upright line was seventeen inches, and the one that crossed it, eight inches long. Small lines were to be seen at the extremity of this latter, and also at the bottom of the upright line, forming crosslets. This old stone, which is still lying there, is five feet long, and measures eighteen inches across the arms. The width of the shaft immediately under the arms is one foot, and it is eight inches in thickness. It has the appearance of a wayside cross, and is certainly not what we should expect to find surmounting a base such as we have examined at Southmead House.

Since I first saw this cross hinges have been put to it, the intention evidently having been to use it again as a gate-post, but it is to be hoped that this design will not be carried out.

In the immediate neighbourhood of Chagford there is very much to interest and delight. He who seeks the beautiful in nature will certainly find it here, and the antiquary may fully occupy his time in the examination of the numerous remains, both pre-historic and mediæval, that abound within a radius of a few miles, including the celebrated dolmen, or cromlech, near Drewsteignton. A point in the lane close by the dolmen, where it is intersected by another, is known as Stone Cross. There is no cross now standing there, but Mr. Ormerod says that he was informed by the occupier of Shilston Farm that many years ago he took an old cross to some place near Sands Gate and made it into a foot-bridge. It is not stated whence this was removed, but as Stone Cross is near at hand it is very probable that it was taken from that spot. It is also stated that another called Stumpy Cross used to stand in the vicinity of Chagford—I have heard Drewston mentioned as being the spot—but I can gain no positive information respecting it.

In the romantic gorge of Fingle, where the scenery is perhaps unsurpassed in Devonshire, the visitor will also find some objects of antiquity, and among them a stone, standing by the wayside, on which is an incised cross. The gorge is somewhat outside the range of country over which our investigations extend, but a notice of the stone seems desirable nevertheless. It will be found beside the zig-zag road that leads from Cranbrook Castle to Fingle Bridge, on the right side in descending, and at a point where a path, of which there are several, diverges from the main one.

Mr. Ormerod took a photograph of this stone in 1863, but it would appear that it was afterwards thrown down, for, writing in 1874, he states that he had not during a few years previous to that date been able to find it. In the same year I also visited the woods, and passed down the road from Cranbrook, but could see nothing of the stone. It has, however, been for a long time replaced. It is about three feet high, and not quite two feet wide. The upright line of the incised cross measures fourteen inches, and the line forming the arms ten inches.

Chagford was one of the four stannary towns of Devon. The others we have already visited—Plympton, Tavistock and Ashburton. In the vicinity remains of tin-streaming operations are extensive.

The church, which is dedicated to St. Michael, was restored in 1865. Some few years after this date the rood-loft stairs were cleared out, when the upper portions of four granite crosses were discovered. These were probably placed here about the commencement of the second half of the sixteenth century, as in a series of accounts of various wardens and guilds of Chagford, there are several entries showing that numerous alterations were then made in the interior of the church.

Leaving Chagford we make our way up the hill by the church to Week Down, where an interesting old cross will claim our attention. The climb is a long one, but we shall be well repaid on reaching the breezy height, by the beautiful view that it commands. The cross comes in sight some time before we reach it, and will be found to be a fine example. It stands within a few yards of the road, but not quite in its original situation, having been removed in 1867, as in consequence of the bank giving way, it was feared it would fall. Another reason there was for its careful preservation; its removal had been contemplated in order to use it for a foot-bridge. That it was saved from such a fate, and that the parish of Chagford was not deprived of an interesting object of antiquity, is a matter for congratulation. It stood formerly on a little higher ground, although it is now nearly on the summit of the down, and can be plainly seen against the sky, as one approaches Chagford by the Moreton road. It was leaning out of the perpendicular before its removal, and was set up inclining at the same angle. It is six and a half feet high, measured down its centre, and the shaft under the arms is fourteen or fifteen inches wide. About midway down this increases to seventeen inches, but again narrows at the bottom. It has very short arms indeed, shorter even than those of the Sourton Cross, as they project barely an inch and a half. They are of unequal size, the southerly being ten inches deep and eleven thick, and the northerly nine inches square. They measure scarcely eighteen inches across, and spring off at a distance of five feet from the ground, on the side that the inclination of the cross causes to be the higher. On each face, in the centre, between the arms, is an incised Maltese cross. That on the eastern has its limbs parallel to the shaft and arms of the cross on which it is graven, but the one on the western face has not. Here the Maltese cross is upright, and a line drawn through it would fall at some little distance from the foot of the old stone. This would seem to show that it was incised after the cross had fallen out of the perpendicular, and though the position of the other does not indicate this, it is probable they were both cut at the same time. The western one is eight and a half inches high, and an inch less than this across, and the eastern nine and a half inches each way. The modern letters, I A, cut very small, are on its northern side. The inclination of the stone is towards the south; it faces almost due east and west. It wears a very venerable look, the head being partly covered with short, grey moss, and forms a pleasing object, standing alone upon this lofty spot.

Ere we leave the down we shall not fail to observe the wondrous prospect commanded from it. To the north-west rises Cosdon, and if we look near its foot we shall descry the roofs of West Week, and be able to trace the greater part of the route we have pursued from that place to Chagford. Lying, as it were, at our feet is Rushford Bridge, and lower down Sandy Park and the entrance to the gorge of Fingle, with Cranbrook further toward the east. In the opposite direction is a wide view of the eastern slopes of the moor, and between Middledon Hill and Nat Tor Down, Kes Tor appears, and we shall never see it to greater advantage.

> "Not proud Olympus yields a nobler sight,
> Though gods assembled grace his towering height,
> Than what more humble mountains offer here,
> Where, in their blessings, all those gods appear."

Just after leaving the common we reach another standing stone, also close by the roadside. This is known locally as Shorter Cross, and to it a history attaches. It was removed in 1873 to Middle Middlecott Farm, not far distant, and placed under a pump there, where it remained buried until 1900. Early in that year, through the instrumentality of Major Yolland, it was disinterred and taken back to its original situation. The stone is six feet in height, and about one foot and a half in breadth. On one of its faces there is a Latin cross in relief, twenty-one inches high, and about eleven inches across the arms. The foot of this is about three feet nine inches from the ground; in its centre a small Greek cross is incised. On the other face of the pillar will be seen an incised Latin cross.

From Shorter Cross we descend to Middlecott, where are three farmhouses, whence our way leads by Thorn. Shortly after passing this farm we enter upon the Moretonhampstead road, and soon reach that border town.

CHAPTER XIV.

From Moretonhampstead to the Western Border Commons.

An Old Road—Cross at Lynscott—Headless Cross—Ancient Guiding Stones—Beetor Cross—A Traditionary Battle—Bennet's Cross—Heath Stone—Newhouse—Story of the Grey Wethers—Meripit Hill—Maggie Cross—Jonas Coaker—Cut Lane—The Lich Path—Clapper Bridges—The Rundle Stone—Long Ash Hill.

The present highway across the moor from Moretonhampstead to Plymouth and Tavistock is formed on the line of an ancient track. The wayside cross, old guide stones, fords and clapper bridges, enable us to trace it, besides which we have seventeenth and early eighteenth century mention of it, as will presently be shown. We shall first briefly notice such objects in and around Moreton as now concern us, and then set out on our journey over this old highway, in order that we may examine others which will prove not less interesting.

The number of crosses in the Dartmoor district already known, has lately been increased by the discovery of two in the neighbourhood of Moreton, by Dr. W. J. Stephens of that town. One was found by him at Lynscott, where it served as a gate-post, and the other at Elsford, in Bovey Tracey Parish. The latter is in the hedge by the side of the road leading from Pepperdon to Hennock, and close to the farm named, which is about a mile and a half from Lustleigh. It is thirty-three inches high, but probably the greater part of the shaft is below the surface of the ground; it also measures the same across the arms. Dr. Stephens has been instrumental in getting the hedge pruned, and the cross is now exposed to view. The cross at Lynscott has been sadly mutilated, one of the arms having been knocked off, presumably to adapt it to the purpose to which it has been put, and the greater part of the head as well. There are also notches in one of its faces, of the kind made to receive the ends of the bars which formerly took the place of hinged gates. Dr. Stephens, whose interest in these memorials of other days does not stop at simply discovering them, brought the matter to the notice of Mr. Charles Cuming, who resides at Lynscott, and he removed the cross to a suitable spot. That its original site was not far distant is evidenced by the name of the field Cross Park at the entrance to which it stood.

The cross is five and a half feet in height, and about eighteen inches across the arms; on one face, between these, is an incised cross, the lines being seven and eleven inches long.

As there is an old track very near by, which leads to Buttern Down and Fingle Bridge, it seems likely that the original purpose of the cross was to mark its direction. Lynscott is about a mile and a half from Moreton.

There is another stone situated at about the same distance from Moreton, but in a different direction. It is known as the Headless Cross, and stands on Mardon Down, not far from the road to Clifford Bridge. It is sometimes called the Maximajor Stone, and in spite of its first-mentioned name, it is doubtful whether it ever was a cross. The stone which is of rude appearance, is six feet in height, about four feet in girth at the base, and about three feet at the top.

Moretonhampstead is locally said to be "twelve miles from everywhere," being about that distance from Exeter, Newton Abbot, Princetown and Okehampton. It is situated amid scenery of the most attractive kind, and as it can be reached by rail forms an easily accessible centre for the visitor. The church, dedicated to St. Andrew, is an ancient structure, and is remarkably well placed. At its eastern end is a field called the Sentry, a corruption of Sanctuary, whence the ground slopes very rapidly, so that from the further side of the depression the building is seen standing on a bold hill, while when approached from the west it will be found to be on the same level as the town. The tower is plain, with that sturdy look so characteristic of those of the moorland district. In the churchyard are a number of very old tombstones, fashioned from the granite of the neighbouring hills.

We shall find the old Moretonhampstead cross just without the south gate of the churchyard, beneath an ancient elm. This tree, so long the glory of Moreton, has had its branches curiously trained, so that the upper portion once assumed a cuplike form, and in this a platform was sometimes laid and dancing took place on it. The following extracts from a journal kept by the great-grandfather of a lady long resident in the town, are interesting as giving us some actual dates upon which festivities took place on the tree.

JUNE 4th, 1800.

His Majesty's birthday. Every mark of loyalty was shewn. In the afternoon a concert of instrumental music was held on the Cross Tree.

AUGUST 28th, 1801.

The Cross Tree floored and seated round, with a platform, railed on each side, from the top of an adjoining garden wall to the tree, and a flight of steps in the garden for the company to ascend. After passing the platform they enter under a grand arch formed of boughs. There is sufficient room for thirty persons to sit around. and six couples to dance, besides the orchestra. From the novelty of this rural apartment it is expected much company will resort there during the summer.

AUGUST 19th, 1807.

This night the French officers* assembled on the Cross Tree, with their band of music. They performed several airs with great taste.

I have been unable to ascertain the date upon which the last dance took place among the boughs of this old elm, but I understand they were not infrequent, and were many of them attended by the guests of a former house of entertainment called the London Inn, and which was near by.

Unfortunately the Cross Tree was greatly injured, in fact partly destroyed, by a storm that took place on the 13th October, 1891, when the force of the wind was so great that the ancient elm could not withstand it, and about a quarter past two o'clock in the afternoon most of the upper part was blown down, carrying with it a large piece of the trunk, which was found to be quite hollow. This latter the late Mr. William Phillips Harvey had replaced and securely fastened, and to his fostering care do we owe it that this historic tree still throws a grateful shade over the venerable cross below.

The shaft of the Moreton cross is missing, and the head and arms are now fixed close to the foot of the old elm, which grows from the centre of a large octagonal base, the sides of which measure thirty-eight, and some forty-eight inches. This is about two and a half feet in height, though owing to the ground

---

*These were prisoners of war residing at Moretonhampstead on parole.

around it being a little uneven, it is in places not quite so much. There is a plinth, the sloping top of which is exactly one foot from a cornice formed by projecting slabs, and is six inches high. From the outer edge of these slabs to the trunk of the tree the distances varies from about twenty-six to thirty-four inches. This is now covered with earth and planted, but we cannot congratulate those responsible for the innovation upon the effect of their work, which violates every principle of good taste, and sadly mars the appearance of the old tree and the venerable stone beneath it.

The cross or what remains of it, rises twenty-one inches above this base, and is fixed in position with cement. This was done by Mr. Harvey, who informed me that there were only about two inches of the stone sunk in the hole formed to receive it. It is octagonal in shape, but the angles are much weathered; the head is forty-six inches in girth, and the arms forty-two, these measuring twenty-seven inches across, and projecting six inches from the shaft. There is an oval-shaped cavity six inches by five, and three in depth, on the head of this cross, and also two little channels, each about an inch in width; around the top of the head are two mouldings. In the centre of one of its faces (that turned from the tree) is a Greek Tau cross, incised to the depth of an inch and a half, the upright limb being a foot high and three inches wide, and the arms ten inches across, and four and a half inches wide. On the other face is a hollow of precisely the same size as the arms of the Greek Tau, but in a similar position to the upright limb of it.

Very near to the Cross Tree is the old poor-house, a building of some interest, having an arcade with ten small arches. five on each side of the entrance.

George Bidder, the eminent engineer, was born at Moretonhampstead. He was placed at the University of Edinburgh when only in his fourteenth year, having developed surprising powers of mental calculation. He was the engineer of several important railways and other great public works. His death took place in 1878.

The highway from Moretonhampstead to the western border commons being formed, as we have already stated, on the line of the ancient track we wish to follow, we shall have the advantage of a good road across the forest.

At the distance of a little over a mile, at a cross-road, we shall notice an old guiding-stone on the left, with the letters M N C T incised, one on each of its four faces. These stand for Moretonhampstead, Newton, Chagford, and Tavistock, and are so placed as to indicate the direction of each. Three miles from Moreton our road is again crossed by another, at a spot known as Watching Place, and also as Beetor Cross, and here, too, we find a similarly inscribed stone, excepting that the direction of Newton is not indicated. Formerly the traveller over this road also saw the spot marked by a stone cross, but for the half century preceding 1900, and perhaps for a longer time, it was missing from its place, its name alone remaining there.

In 1848 the Rev. Samuel Rowe stated that Beetor Cross was then standing in a field adjoining the spot that bears its name. In 1857 Mr. Ormerod made a drawing of it, when it was acting as a gate-post on Hele Moors. This is probably the same spot on which it stood in Mr. Rowe's time, as Hele Moors, which are now, and were then, enclosed, are close by, and may very well be described as fields. Mr. Ormerod informs us in his paper, written in 1874, that three years before "it was removed from that spot to act in the same capacity at a gateway leading out of Hele Plantation to Hele House." I think he is hardly correct here, as I made enquiry some years ago from those likely to know, and I could not find that the cross ever formed a gate-post at Hele Plantation. In 1892 I saw it when it acted as a gate-post in a field to the south of the road, and there it remained until the last year of the nineteenth century

Early in that year the Rev. W. H. Thornton, rector of North Bovey, brought the subject of its restoration to the notice of the members of the Teign Naturalists' Field Club, and a sum of money to defray the cost of the desirable work was voted. It was carried out by Mr. Thornton, with the co-operation of the owner, Mr. Taylor, of Hele, and in the month of August was completed. A party of forty-five members of the club drove to the spot to inspect the cross and afterwards visited the rectory where the pleasing ceremony of its inauguration was concluded

That this old cross, now happily nearer the site on which it probably stood for centuries, was erected to mark the ancient track across the moor, seems to be likely, though it is possible it may also have commemorated some event. Tradition assigns its erection solely to the latter, and relates that it was set up to mark the scene of a conflict between the invading Saxon and the Christian British of the moor. But whatever may have been the intentions of those who reared it in the dim past, it is gratifying to reflect that one, at least, is fulfilled; that the symbol of the Christian faith here meets the eye of the wayfarer.

There is also another tradition connected with this spot. It is related that here was erected the gibbet on which a criminal was hung in chains, the last in the neighbourhood to be made an example of by a barbarous law.

Beetor cross is very rudely fashioned, and on Hele Moors stood but a little over four feet in height; the breadth of the shaft is about eleven inches, and its thickness an inch less. Across the arms, one of which has a corner broken off, the measurement is sixteen inches, so that it will be seen that they project but little. The head is not so wide as the shaft, and one of the arms is somewhat higher than the other. On its face is an incised cross, which, however, can only be seen when the sun is shining upon it, and the ends of the lines appear to have had cross strokes, forming crosslets.

One mile beyond Beetor Cross we enter upon the moor, and about a mile and a half further on shall come in sight of another old wayside cross. It stands near the road on the left as we advance, and it will be seen that it is leaning consideraby out of the perpendicular, but is yet in a perfect condition. It is of very rugged appearance, no pains having been taken in forming the shaft, this seeming to be little more than the stone left in its natural shape, the short, rudely-carved arms, and the head, being the only parts in which any attempt at fashioning is displayed.

It is known as Bennet's Cross, and though we are ignorant why this name was bestowed upon it, we can, at all events, be sure that it has borne it for at least two centuries. I find the cross mentioned by that name in the deposition of William French, of Widecombe, in an action brought by the rector of Lydford for tithes, in 1702, and as it appears that it was then well-known, it is more than probable that it had been so called for some time prior to that date.

It is six feet in height on one side, and nearly eight inches more than this on the other, the ground being there worn away, and the arms are one foot nine inches across. The girth of the shaft is much greater at the bottom than at its upper part; above the arms it slightly tapers, as also do the arms themselves. On the west-north-west face, that which fronts the road, the modern letters W B are incised; these stand for "Warren Bounds," the cross forming one of the boundaries of Headland Warren, and similar letters will also be noticed on several other stones near by which define its limits. The cross is also a boundary mark of the parishes of North Bovey and Chagford, and of the land over which extend the rights belonging to Vitifer Mine.*

A few loose stones will be observed near Bennet's Cross, being the marks of the tin-bounds, which are renewed once a year. These stones are then placed, as the country-people have it, "brandis-wise;" that is, in the form of a brandis, the name by which the triangular stands on which kettles are set on the hearth are called.

Whether Bennet's Cross was originally erected to mark a boundary, or the path we are pursuing, cannot, of course, be determined. The probability is that it was designed for both purposes; that a guide to the track being necessary it was decided to set up the cross in a situation where it would not only act as such, but define the parish boundaries at this point as well.

In the vicinity of Bennet's Cross the ancient road from Chagford joined the one from Moreton, the former being marked near here by a monolith referred to in the records of the forest as Heath Stone. This is also shown as defining the road on a small map in a book published in 1720, being an improved edition by John Owen, of the Middle Temple, of a former work by Ogilby. In it our road across the forest is

---

* Nearly all the Dartmoor warrens are situated either in the neighbourhood of Newhouse, or in the Plym valley. Huntingdon, which we have already noticed, is one of the exceptions. In speaking of the bridge there (p. 19 *ante*) I inadvertently stated that the warren was formed early in the eighteenth century. This should have been the nineteenth. The information I obtained about thirty years ago from Mr. Michelmore, a grandson of the first encloser, and who then resided there. It was taken in from the forest in 1808.

shown, with a branch to Plymouth from Two Bridges, as at the present day. As the existing highway was not made till after 1772, that which is shown by Owen was, of course, only a rough track.

Proceeding on our way we soon arrive at Newhouse, or as it is now called, the Warren House Inn, a small wayside hostelry. Before the present house was built the old inn stood on the opposite side of the road, but it has been pulled down for many years. It was generally regarded as the scene of the story, related by Mrs. Bray, of a traveller who discovered a corpse in a chest in the chamber to which he had retired for the night, and whose terror was only dispelled in the morning, when he learned the meaning of so strange a circumstance. The deep snow had prevented its removal for burial, so the expedient had been adopted of preserving it in salt in the old chest. I have heard it said that on the morning after his adventure the traveller called at Prince Hall and related what he had seen.

A story which I gathered many years ago on the moor shows us that the dwellers in this out-of-the-way region are by no means averse to indulging in a practical joke. A farmer, who was unacquainted with the neighbourhood, being at Newhouse with several moormen, was induced by a man whom he happened to meet there to agree to the purchase of what he imagined to be a flock of sheep. He afterwards found that the seller, an individual named Debben, had got the best of the bargain. The old ballad tells us how Robin Hood, disguised as a butcher, once decoyed the Sheriff of Nottingham to the glades of Sherwood Forest, under pretence of selling him some horned cattle, but which turned out to be the king's deer; in the present instance, however, the supposed sheep were found to be in reality nothing more than granite stones. Near Siddaford Tor, in this vicinity, are two circles known as the Grey Wethers, formed of upright stones, of which several have, unfortunately, been taken away. It seems that the victim of the joke, who was unaware of the existence of these circles, was offered so many grey wethers at such a price, being told that he might see them if he wished, for they were "up in the new-take, near Siddaford Tor." On the bargain being made he was filled with chagrin at discovering what it was he had engaged to purchase.

Resuming our walk along the highway we shortly cross Statsford Bridge, and ascend Meripit Hill. In July, 1831 Mr. Bray observed a fallen cross here, lying near a circular pit, close to the road on the left, as he was going towards Post Bridge. It was nine feet and three-quarters in length, and its arms were very short; but it was of a regular shape, and better wrought than the crosses generally seen on the moor.

I find that on the map in Owen's book what certainly seems to be the object seen by Mr. Bray, is shown. It is there marked as " a stone called Merry Pit," and is placed on the same side of the road as that on which the cross was observed.

From Jonas Coaker, who was well known as the Dartmoor Poet, and who died in 1890 at the age of 89, I gathered some particulars concerning this cross, for without doubt it was to this particular stone that he referred. He said that he remembered a cross on Meripit Hill, which was afterwards removed to Post Bridge, which is about a mile distant, and used as a post for the toll-gate on the latter being erected there. When the gate was abolished, but, if we remember rightly, before the toll-house was pulled down, the posts were removed. I have, however, never been able to learn what became of them, nor to discover the remains of the cross.

This instance of wanton spoliation—one among the many that have taken place on the moor—is not only to be regretted, but arouses one's indignation. Stone is here in abundance, but in order that a little labour might be saved, an ancient relic has been lost to us.

On arriving at the moorland settlement of Post Bridge, we shall notice on the right hand side of the road a gateway, with a cottage, which was intended for a lodge to Stannon House, which building, however, was never finished in the manner. contemplated, but was turned into a labourer's dwelling, Here, close to the lodge gate, formerly stood a cross, but no one recollects it now. Jonas Coaker said that it was known as Maggie Cross, and that he remembered it, but was unable to say what had become of it.

In the entry in Mr. Bray's Journal* concerning the cross on Meripit Hill, mention is also made of another that he saw

---

* *Tamar and Tavy*, vol. i, p. 299

on the same day at Post Bridge. This, he says, was near the bridge and close to the road. That it was the cross which Jonas Coaker remembered, there can be no doubt.

Crossing the modern bridge, and noticing just below it the old clapper bridge, which is named in Owen's book, and which is the finest example of these structures now existing on the moor, we proceed for a few score yards on the road, when we shall observe a turning on our right, where a rough track, called Drift Lane, runs up by the side of the Dart. There are traces of an ancient path on the moor in a line with this road, and it is very probably a part of it. The latter is known as Cut Lane, and led from the valley of the Dart over the northern shoulder of Cut Hill, and the combe under Fur Tor to the north-eastern and northern borders of the moor.

In 1260 Bishop Bronescombe, at the request of the inhabitants of the villages of Balbeny and Pushyll in the forest, permitted them to pay certain of their tithes to Widecombe, where they worshipped, their parish church of Lydford being at such a distance from them. That Cut Lane, as it is now called, was one of the paths used by the inhabitants of the villages named when it became necessary to visit their mother church, there is no doubt. It is marked in places by stones, but there is no cross to be found upon it, though I have some reason for thinking that one did formerly point out its direction.

Another track in this part of the moor is the Lich Path, referred to in Chapter xi., and said to have been used for the purpose of carrying the dead to the churchyard at Lydford for burial. It is plainly to be traced in many places, but throughout its course I have never been able to find a solitary cross, though, as in the case of Cut Lane, I have grounds for believing that one, at least, once existed upon it.

Our road to the western precincts of the forest will next lead us to Two Bridges, where is now a county bridge spanning the West Dart. Not far above it, on the Cowsic, is a clapper, and it is said that one also formerly existed on the Dart further down the stream.

Near the western end of the bridge the road divides, one branch, as already stated, leading to Plymouth, the other to Tavistock. The old track to the latter town seems to have kept a little to the northward of the line of the present road, a ruined clapper on the Blackabrook, close to Fice's Well, to which we have already alluded, indicating its direction. But some two hundred years ago the track seems to have run just as the present road does. On Owen's map one of the objects marking the route from Two Bridges to Tavistock is a "Great stone call'd Roundle." Now the Rundle Stone until a few years ago stood by the side of the highway, on the boundary line of the forest, which line it was mentioned as marking in 1702. From this it seems certain that the path which crossed the Blackabrook by the clapper at Fice's Well had given place at the beginning of the eighteenth century to the track on which the modern road was formed.

The Rundle Stone was a pillar, seven feet in height and four in girth. On one of its faces, near the top, the letter R was cut in relief; this was seven inches high. For some time I saw it being used as a gate-post, and it was afterwards to be seen lying by the wall close by. Now it has disappeared, and I can glean no tidings of it. It has left its name upon the spot where it stood for so long, and that is all that remains to us of this old way-mark.

In the chapter on the Abbots' Way it was stated that a later path was formed upon that old road throughout its course from Long Ash Hill to Whitchurch Down.* At this part of it we have now again arrived, and shall find that such is proved by the existence of several guide stones on the former hill, of a period subsequent to the time of the monks. These have the letter A on one side of them and T on the other, denoting that they point the way to Ashburton and to Tavistock. This track is in a line, or nearly so, with that which we have mentioned as being formed by the menhir above Merivale, the Windypost, and the cross on Whitchurch Down.†

The road we have followed from Moreton is referred to in a document of an earlier date than that of Owen's edition of Ogilby's book. Mr. R. N. Worth in a paper on *Men and Manners in Stuart Plymouth*,‡ gives a number of extracts

---

* p. 80, *ante*. The track from Moreton, and from Ashburton, joined the ancient Abbots' Way near the Rundle Stone, if the latter path ran, as we have supposed, to the eastward of North Hisworthy Tor. Jobbers' Cross was also in the vicinity, and it is not unlikely was the point where the paths met. † p. 80, *ante*.

‡ *Trans. Devon Assoc.*, vol. xv. p. 475.

from the Municipal Records of that borough, among which occurs the following :—

1699-1700

Item paid towards defraying the charges of putting vpp Morrestones on Dartmoor in the way leading from Plymouth towards Exon for guideing of Travellers passing that way the sume of £2.

Having thus followed the Moreton road to the western purlieus of the forest, and noticed the objects on it which have called us so far, we here leave it at the point where its early forerunner probably joined the way of the monks that led to Tavistock, and retrace our steps towards the town whence we set out.

Just after passing Moor Gate, where we enter on the enclosed lands at the fourth milestone from Moreton, a turning on the right, or south side of the road, will be observed. Here a path leads across two fields to Leeper, a border farm, where the upper portion of a fine cross was recently found. As it had been built into the wall of the garden in such a manner as to expose its face, its existence was, of course, known to the dwellers at the farm, but little or no notice had ever been taken of the stone by them. It is three feet four inches high, and one foot ten inches across the arms, one of which has been broken and is very short. The width of the shaft is about fifteen inches, and the arms are eleven inches deep. There is a Latin cross in relief placed in the centre, twenty-five inches high and twelve and-a-half inches across the arms, the limbs being three inches wide. Whether this cross originally marked the track we have pursued across the forest, or a path between Beetor Cross and the Challacombe Valley, or a branch to Widecombe, cannot, of course, be determined. It is a fine example, and judging from its present proportions was, when complete, not less than six feet high.

CHAPTER XV.

Crosses on the Bovey River.

Horse Pit Cross—An Old-time Village—North Bovey Cross—Cross at Hele—Tradition of a Chapel by the Stream—Disappearance of the Manaton Cross—Its Socket-stone—Cross at South Harton Gate—Cross Park—The Bishop's Stone—Inscribed Stone at Lustleigh—Crosses at Bovey Tracey—Cross at Sanduck.

In the parishes of North Bovey, Lustleigh and Bovey Tracey, which are watered by a tributary of the Teign, from which the first and last of those places derive their names, are several crosses, and these will now claim our attention.

Moretonhampstead will again become our starting-place, and we shall leave the town by the North Bovey road. About a mile from it we reach a point where this road is crossed by another, and shall here find an old stone cross standing a few feet from the hedge. An adjoining field is known as Horse Pit, and this name has been bestowed upon the venerable stone. It is barely three-and-a-half feet high, and it is possible that a portion of the bottom part of the shaft may be missing. Across the arms, which are one foot in depth, the measurement is twenty-two inches; the shaft is nine inches thick, and a little more than this in width. On one face—which looks S.E. by S.—it has the letter **N**, and on the other the letter **O**, standing respectively for Newton and Okehampton. At the end of the arm pointing in the direction of Moretonhampstead, is an **M**, and in a similar position on the other, a **B**, showing the traveller the way to North Bovey. These letters are incised.

The village of North Bovey, which we shall soon reach from Horse Pit Cross, presents a very charming picture, and one that impresses the visitor as being truly English in all its features. The houses are grouped around a grove of noble old oaks, and as we stand beneath their boughs and look about us we shall note with pleasure that among the usual accompaniments of a rural settlement, the village can boast of its ancient cross. It is true that for a time this was unkindly, or thoughtlessly, banished from its proper place, and made to serve the purpose of a foot-bridge over a rivulet that falls into the Bovey Brook a short distance below the village, but this we are willing to forgive at seeing it once more standing erect, in, or near, its original situation. To the Rev. J. P. Jones, a gentleman whose writings prove him to have been possessed of true antiquarian tastes, do we owe the preservation of this old memorial of other times. He caused it to be brought from the rivulet, and after having the base, or socket-stone, which had been cast on one side, set firmly in the ground, had the cross fixed upon it. This was done not long after the passing of "An Act for the Relief of His Majesty's Roman Catholic Subjects," in April, 1829, Mr. Jones then being the curate of North Bovey. Whether this piece of legislation was instrumental in bringing about a decision to restore this cross, or whether the time chosen was merely accidental, I am not able to say.

The cross is five feet two inches in height, the shaft being fourteen inches in width at the bottom, and nine-and-a-half inches in thickness; immediately under the arms it is an inch wider. Across the arms the measurement is twenty-five inches; one of these projects four, and the other five-and-a-half inches, and they spring off at a distance of three feet eleven inches from the bottom. The head rises five-and-a-half inches above them. Four small iron clamps secure the shaft in the socket, which is much too large for it, from which circumstance it has been supposed that the cross did not originally belong to the base. But from what I was once able to gather from an old inhabitant of the village, who remembered very well when the cross was re-erected, it does not appear that such a belief existed at the time. The workmanship in each is plain, and of precisely similar character, and apart from the size of the socket they certainly seem intended for one another. It is possible that the socket may have been enlarged in order to permit of the cross being set nearer to the centre of the stone, or the foot of the shaft may have been shaped like one we shall presently notice at South Harton Farm, in the parish of Lustleigh, and this would necessitate a very large socket. The base-stone is fourteen inches high, and very nearly three feet square at the bottom, but gathered into an octagon at the top. One of its corners is broken off.

From North Bovey we shall proceed to Hele, making our way thither by descending to the higher bridge over the Bovey Brook, and following the lane that leads by Yard Farm. As we approach Hele House, which is about a mile and a half from North Bovey, we shall see the cross standing high above the road on our right, and shall at once perceive that it is an exceedingly fine example. It is a Maltese cross, and the arms and shaft are octagonal. The base in which it is set is a stone ten inches high, rectangular at the bottom, and measuring thirty-six by twenty-nine inches, but at the top formed into an octagon. The cross is five feet ten inches in height, the lower part of the shaft being square, but assuming the octagonal form one foot from the bottom. At this point it is forty-two inches in girth, and this diminishes to thirty-seven inches immediately under the arms; close to the shaft these are one inch less than this in girth. They spring off at the height of four feet five inches from the bottom, and measure twenty-five inches across. The head rises seven inches above them.

A tradition exists in the neighbourhood that a small chapel once stood close to the stream which runs just below, and that from there the cross was brought. Around it pilgrims were wont to gather ere setting out across the moor to visit the abbey of Tavistock, and to offer prayers in the little shrine.

Hele Cross stands upon masonry raised to the height of several feet. Mr. Ormerod seeing that it was in danger of being undermined through a hollow having been scooped out close to it by persons taking away gravel, called the attention of those interested in its preservation to the matter, and in 1868 it was moved back a little and fixed in its present position, and secured by a clamp, by a mason of North Bovey. This was done, I have been informed, at the expense of the late Earl of Devon.

Retracing our steps we shall pass near the village of North Bovey, and so make our way by the lane and some pleasant path-fields to Manaton. Here the well-kept green, bordered with trees, will at once attract the attention of the visitor, while he will also not fail to be struck with the romantic surroundings.

A cross formerly stood in Manaton churchyard, but the base of it alone remains. One day, to the surprise of the inhabitants, it was found to have been removed, but where, or by whom, they could not at first discover. At length it began to be rumoured that it had been taken away by no less a person than the rector himself, and for the reason that the people had made a practice when bringing their dead for burial of carrying the corpse thrice round the cross before taking it into the church. This custom did not commend itself to the rector, the Rev. John Charles Carwithen, whose influence over his flock, one would imagine, could not have been very great, or he would certainly have been able to dissuade them from the performance of so meaningless a ceremony. It is very certain he could not have possessed much reverence for antiquities, or he would have hesitated to commit such an act of vandalism as to rob Manaton of its cross. Mr. Carwithen, who was instituted in 1841, and remained in the parish until 1848, was the eighth rector of that name.

But the discovery of Iconoclast is one thing: the finding the place where he has hidden his broken images another. Manaton Cross has never been seen since the night the rector removed it. Old William Derges, a former sexton, remembered the searches for the missing cross. It was thought that it might have been buried, and all likely spots were carefully probed, the result, however, being nothing but disappointment. The rector had done his work too well.

The base of the cross, which is near the south-east corner of the chancel, is of granite, measuring thirty-two inches by thirty, and having its surface level with the turf. The socket is rather over fourteen inches square, and five inches deep.

Crossing the green and passing in front of the rectory with its old granite gateway, we proceed a short distance up the lane, and then strike over some path-fields on the right. In a few minutes we shall reach the edge of a wood, clothing the steep side of a valley, across which rises a rock-strewn hill, and over this our way lies. Descending the hill, through the wood to Foxworthy, we speedily find ourselves in the renowned Lustleigh Cleave. Passing a pile of rocks that we see midway up the acclivity on the left, we leave the path, and after a rather toilsome climb, gain the summit. Not far from a plantation is one of the entrances to South Harton Farm, and if we can obtain permission to pass that way it will shorten the distance to the object we are desirous of reaching. Beyond the court a private road leads to the main entrance gate, and immediately without this, and built into the wall, on the left as we emerge, will be seen an ancient cross. It has been split down the centre to form a pair of gate-posts, but the parts are now fitted neatly together. There is no attempt at any ornamentation, but it is a good example of a plain wayside cross, and to Mr. Wills, a former occupier of South Harton, who placed it here for preservation, the antiquary, and indeed all who delight to find these relics of the past by our highways and in our quiet lanes, must feel indebted. Its total height is six feet three inches, and the height to the arms four feet ten inches. These measure twenty inches across, and project about three inches from the shaft. The thickness of the latter is thirteen inches, except at its foot, where it is greater; it is also rather wider there than immediately under the arms. It is possible that the lower part of the shaft of the cross at North Bovey was fashioned in a similar manner, and if so the size of the socket is explained.

We turn up the lane on the left hand, but soon bending round to the right shall proceed to Higher Coombe farmhouse. Passing this and arriving at the gate opening on the parish road, we shall observe another gate immediately opposite. Through this a field called Cross Park is entered, and near its centre we shall perceive a cross fixed upon a granite rock. This formerly stood in the bank near by and was placed in its present situation in 1860, by Mr. Amery, who then occupied the farm. On approaching it we shall find it to consist of the upper portion only, a great part of the shaft being missing. It is twenty-eight inches high; its width eleven inches, and its thickness nine. The arms, one of which has a small piece broken off from it, are twenty-three inches across, and above them the head rises nine inches. The cross is carefully secured in its place by four small iron clamps. It is gratifying to find that, like the cross at South Harton, this interesting object has not been cast aside or destroyed. From Cross Park a walk of about a mile will bring us to Lustleigh.

By the roadside, and very near to the railway station, a large block of granite may be seen, raised above the level of the ground, and built into a modern wall. It has been suggested that it is the pedestal of a cross, and this is not improbable. There is no socket cut in it, but upon it may have been placed the stone in which the cross was set. It is two feet in height, and the lower part is square, but having the corners chamfered, the side facing the road measuring just over three feet. Fourteen inches from the bottom the corners are cut away, forming the top into an octagon, the sides of which are seventeen and eighteen inches across. It is known as the Bishop's Stone, and some faint carving on one of its sides is said to represent the arms of Bishop Grandisson, who, according to a tradition, dined upon it, when passing on one occasion through Lustleigh. But there seems to be a better explanation of its name; it is probable that the stone once marked the boundary of some episcopal possessions. The late Mr. J. B. Davidson in a paper relating to a document now in the Albert Memorial Museum at Exeter, setting forth some ancient boundaries in this and adjoining parishes, suggests that this stone, or an inscribed stone that is now in the south porch of Lustleigh Church, is one of the bond-marks named in the manuscript the Writelan Stone. He states that he considers it probable that the lands comprehended within the boundaries mentioned on the document were in some way connected with the See of Exeter, one fact tending to confirm this supposition being that the ancient piece of writing was found among the Cathedral archives. If then the tract of land in question was really so connected, it would seem more likely that the granite block now known as the Bishop's stone is identical with the Writelan Stone, than that we see this old boundary mark in the stone at the church.

The latter is laid across the south entrance, a situation from which it certainly ought to be rescued, as although it is now kept covered by a mat in order that the characters upon it may not be utterly effaced, it is by no means one likely to aid in its preservation. The inscription upon it has been read as CATVIDOC CONRINO, but some of the letters are not very distinct.

From Lustleigh we shall proceed to Bovey Tracey by the road connecting Moretonhampstead with that town, and just as we enter it shall notice the lower portion of the shaft of a cross, fixed in a base of granite, and standing on some masonry several feet above the roadway. It is partly built into the wall of a garden belonging to Cross Cottage, and near a lane leading to a farm called Higher Atway. Dr. Croker, who has left us some geological notices of the district, as well as a brief account of the eastern part of Dartmoor, placed the cross where we see it now, as the widening of the road many years since necessitated its removal from its original situation. Both the piece of shaft and the socket-stone are of very plain workmanship, and are much weathered. The former, which is thirty-four inches high, is sixteen inches wide at the bottom, and its corners are slightly chamfered. The latter measures about four-and-a-half feet across. There is a small incised cross on the shaft which, it is plainly to be seen, is comparatively modern. It is said to have been placed on it when the stone was built into the wall.

Formerly the day on which the portreeve of Bovey is chosen was observed as a holiday, and was known as Mayor's Monday, as it fell upon the first Monday after the 3rd of May. It was the practice in former times for the " Mayor of Bovey " on these festive occasions to ride round this cross and strike it with a stick.

The market cross of Bovey, which stands in the middle of the town, is a striking object, particularly when approached by the road leading from the bridge. It stands upon a base and pedestal of two steps, but previous to 1865 was not in its present situation. It, however, stood close by, and was moved in order to make room for a new Town Hall. The pedestal is raised upon a modern foundation, which forms as it were a lower stage, and consisting of blocks of cut granite, square at the bottom, but with the corners steeply sloped, so that its top is octagonal, which is the form the steps of the pedestal take. These steps are about eighteen inches in height, each having a moulding at the top, very much worn and broken, and the lower one a chamfered plinth. The base or socket-stone is three feet ten inches square at the bottom, and gathered into an octagon at the top. It is nineteen-and-a-half inches high. Upon this is fixed the shaft, which like the socket-stone is square at the bottom, but a short distance up the angles are chamfered, and it becomes octagonal. It is of a tapering form, and about eight feet high. On this, as the original was missing, is fixed a head of modern workmanship, the gift of the Hon. Canon Courtenay. The design is good, and thoroughly in keeping with the old shaft. It was cut by a stone-mason of the town named Treleaven.

From Bovey Town Cross we shall pass up the hill to the outskirts, where the church is situated. Entering the churchyard by the south gate we shall perceive on our right a very handsome cross, upon which it is impossible to look without feelings of mingled regret and pleasure. Regret at noticing that but little of the original cross remains, and pleasure when we see what good results a careful and judicious "restoration" may effect. Though only the lower portion of the shaft and one of the arms of the old cross were to be found, so well has the work of supplying the parts that were deficient been executed, that we can feel confident we see in what has been produced a perfect counterpart of the old Bovey churchyard cross. The shaft being of a tapering form, and an arm existing, its proportions could, with the exercise of care, be accurately determined; this trouble was not grudged, and the result is most happy.

The late Earl of Devon, when Lord Courtenay, discovered the fragments of the old cross serving the purpose of a step at the churchyard gate. They were removed, and the cross was set up near the east end of the church. Being thrown down it was again set up, but was once more overturned. Lord Courtenay then obtained permission to remove it to Powderham as a trust, where it was repaired and fixed upon a pedestal. When the Hon. Canon Courtenay became vicar of Bovey, the Earl of Devon mentioned the above circumstance to him, and the cross was then brought back and re-erected in the churchyard. This account of the discovery and "restoration" of Bovey churchyard cross was furnished to Mr. Ormerod by Canon Courtenay.

The base in which the cross is set is one foot high, with chamfered angles, standing upon a pedestal of three low steps, and octagonal in form. It is a Maltese cross, and the angles are chamfered. Its height is exactly six feet.

It will thus be seen that the little town of Bovey Tracey can boast of three erect crosses. Neither of them occupies precisely its original position, but at the same time has not lacked kindly aid to its preservation.

On each side of the south porch of Bovey Tracey Church is a large flat granite stone, laid upon the low bank bordering the path to form a sort of coping. One is six-and-a-half feet long, and the other, a little less, while in width they are both two feet three inches. They have each a very large cross incised upon them in outline, with a rectangular base bearing lines cut in relief. Of these lines two cross diagonally, and intersect each other in the centre, while an upright line also cuts through the centre, so that the device bears a resemblance to the stripes on the national flag of the Royal navy. It is also similar to the lower half of the monogram usually known as the cross of Constantine.

The extensive plain of Bovey Heathfield lies to the south of the town, and it is stated in *Letters, Historical and Botanical, relating to places in the Vale of Teign*, by Dr. Fraser Halle, which appeared in 1851, that tradition pointed to it as the spot where a conflict took place between the troops of Cromwell, who was there in person, and the royalist brigade under Lord Wentworth, resulting in the defeat of the latter. A granite pillar, which when the Rev. J. P. Jones wrote his *History of Teignbridge* (which has not been published) was used as a gate-post, was said to mark the spot where one of the officers was buried, and to be the remains of an ancient cross.

A cross has recently been discovered at Sanduck, a farm in the district with which this chapter deals. In order to include it in the ramble we have just sketched, it would be a good plan to visit that place after leaving South Harton Gate, whence, without retracing our steps, we could make our way to Higher Coombe. The Sanduck Cross was found in the foundations of the farmhouse which was burnt down in April, 1901, on the day of the annual harrier hunt meet on Bellaford Tor. It is a small cross, with chamfered corners, and of elegant proportions.

CHAPTER XVI.

Widecombe-in-the-Moor and the Crosses in its Neighbourhood.

Ilsington—Bag Tor Mill—Cross on Rippon Tor—Cross in Buckland Churchyard—Wayside Cross at Buckland—Dunstone—Cross in Vicarage Garden at Widecombe—Base of Cross on Widecombe Green—Crosses in the Churchyard—Thunder Storm of 1638—Hameldon and its Barrows—Hameldon Cross—The Coffin Stone—Dartmeet—Ouldsbroom Cross—Cross Furzes—Dean Prior—Ancient Track to Plympton—Conclusion.

Our investigations will now take us to that part of Dartmoor lying to the eastward of the Webburn, a tributary of the Dart, where the long valley of Widecombe thrusts itself far up into the moorlands, and our first point will be the summit of Rippon Tor, a lofty eminence in the parish of Ilsington.

From Bovey we may make our way to the common crowned by the granite bosses of Hey Tor, or, if we prefer it, we may pass through pleasant lanes to Brimley and thence to Ilsington village, from which place we can also conveniently gain the down. Mr. Charles Worthy in his *Ashburton and its Neighbourhood*, published in 1875, in noticing Ilsington Church, refers to a block of granite on its south side, which he says "may possibly be the remains of the ancient churchyard cross." This, however, appears to be a mistake. I have carefully searched for it, but could not discover any such stone, and the Rev. Thomas Hales, the late vicar, told me that he had never known of the base of a cross there.

On reaching the common we shall see the fine frontier hill we are about to scale rising boldly before us. When we have accomplished our task, we shall discover, at a distance of only thirty yards from the top of the cairn which crowns the hill, the object which has attracted us hither—a granite cross. I am indebted for my knowledge of this venerable relic to Mr. Spence Bate, not having noticed it on the tor before my attention was drawn to it by his account.* It is totally unlike

---

* *Inscribed Stones*, etc. Trans. Plymouth Institut, vol. vi.

any other of the Dartmoor examples, inasmuch as it could never have been intended to be set up, for it is simply cut in relief on the surface of a large block of granite. It is six feet eight inches long, the breadth of the shaft being fifteen inches The bottom of the shaft seems to have been broken, as also does one of the arms, while the other is not very clearly cut. It stands out in relief about six inches from the surface of the rock on which it is carved.

From its situation near the summit of a tor, this cross, as Mr. Spence Bate observes, was evidently not intended as a mark to any path, "as most of the moorland crosses undoubtedly were." His opinion is that this symbol of the Christian faith was carved at a time when this sign was held to be all powerful in freeing from evil those places where the mysterious rites of Pagan superstition had been observed, and that Rippon Tor may have been such a spot.

Descending from the tor in a northerly direction to Hemsworthy Gate, which opens on the Chagford road, we shall find within a few yards of it, in a corner formed by newtake walls, an object which will have an interest for us.

The late Mr. Robert Dymond, of Exeter, and Blackslade in the parish of Widecombe, having been kind enough to call my attention to the fact that in the perambulation of his manor of Dunstone, this corner, which forms one of the boundary points, is named Stittleford's Cross, I made search on the spot for the purpose of ascertaining whether any traces of such an object were to be found there. I was unsuccessful in discovering a cross of the ordinary character, but found a stone fixed firmly in the ground, and forming part of the wall, bearing a small incised cross, with the letters R M immediately underneath it. The stone stands nearly three and a half feet above the ground, and is sixteen inches wide, the lines of the cross each being six inches, which also is the height of the letters.

On communicating what I had observed to Mr. Dymond, he expressed his belief that the lettters were the initials of Rawlin Mallock, who more than a century ago, laid claims to the lordship of the manor.

It is not unlikely that this stone was erected on the spot where an ancient cross once stood, but which had disappeared in all but the name at the time of the erection of the present boundary mark. Being near the junction of roads, the place is precisely such as we should expect to find chosen as the site of one.

The name is somewhat similar to that of the farm of Chittleford, in the immediate vicinity, but whether it be a corruption of it or not, I am unable to say.

We now turn southward, following the Ashburton road for about a mile and a quarter to Cold East Cross. On the way we pass the ruined walls of Newhouse, which when Rowe wrote his *Perambulation* was a small hostelry. Then striking over the common on the right, we shall descend upon the retired hamlet of Buckland-in-the-Moor ; or, if we prefer it, may follow the road to that place, which will take us by Welstor Cross. We shall find that Buckland can furnish us with more than one example of the objects in quest of which our steps have brought us to this quarter of the moorlands. Laid as a coping stone on the low wall of the churchyard, quite close to the south gate, is the upper portion of the octagonal shaft of a cross, with the head and one of the arms. Owing to its being covered in part with ivy, no accurate measurements of it can be taken, but the fragment is about two feet in length. Just without the gate, and built of granite stones, of which many have a coating of moss, is what was perhaps the pedestal of this cross, though from the size of the sycamore tree that now grows in its centre it is certain that a very long period must have elapsed since it stood there. Its shape is octagonal ; it measures over ten feet across, and each of its sides from four feet to four feet and a few inches. Its height is about twenty-two inches, and the slabs composing its top project and form a cornice.

The little church of Buckland-in-the-Moor is an ancient structure, and possesses several interesting features. It is a daughter church to Ashburton, and is so described in Bishop Lacy's Register of the year 1420. The manor was given by Roger of Buckland to Tor Abbey about the beginning of the thirteenth century.

The other example is not far distant. It is a rude cross built into the wall of the lawn at Buckland, between the entrance doors and the higher gate. At some period it has been used as a gate-post, as is shown by a broken hole, evidently drilled to receive a hinge. One shoulder slightly protrudes from the face of the wall, as it is not squarely built in, while the other is hidden. It partakes of the character of a wayside cross.

The scenery in the neighbourhood of this secluded settlement is of the most attractive character. In the valley the Dart, fresh from the rugged hills, flows between the Buckland Woods and Holne Chase, the paths above the river's banks opening up a constant succession of beauties, while from the hill above many a noble tor may be seen lifting its granite crest in the still air.

A walk of about a mile and a half will bring us to Cockingford, where we cross the East Webburn, as it comes down from Widecombe, to which place we shall now proceed.

Just before reaching the village we shall pass by the hamlet of Dunstone, where, on the green, is a large block of granite, from which it has been thought the place may possibly have taken its name. Here, in former times, the manor courts were held, and the chief rents were deposited in a hollow on this stone. The late Mr. Dymond resolved to revive this custom, and about twenty years ago an open-air court was held here.

Close by the stone a cross formerly stood, but was removed many years ago by the Rev. J. H. Mason, who was vicar of Widecombe from 1815 till his death in 1860, and placed by him for preservation in the vicarage garden.* It is now fixed at the end of a low wall, and over the lower portion of the shaft some ivy has spread itself, as if to shelter

---

* While it is pleasing to find that this ancient cross has been preserved, it is at the same time much to be regretted that it was considered necessary to remove it from its original site, and to erect it in a private garden, where none can see it except as a favour. In the case of the Lynscott Cross, described on page 140, it is satisfactory to note that this time-worn stone has been re-erected on the nearest suitable spot to that at which it was found serving as a gate-post. The work has been accomplished while the preceding sheets were passing through the press· The cross now stands on a bank close to the ancieut highway, and a little on the Moreton side of the field in which Dr. Stephens discovered it. It now stands about five-and-a-half feet high, and is placed so that the face on which is the incised cross is seen from the road. That there was also an incised cross on the other face becomes evident when the stone is closely examined, but in sinking the holes for the bars the markings have in great part been destroyed. The Lynscott Cross forms a pleasing object by the wayside, and antiquaries will feel indebted to Dr. Stephens for calling attention to it, aud urging the desirability of its removal and re-erection, and to Mr. Charles Cuming for promptly recognising this in so practical a manner.

the grey old relic from the rude blasts of the neighbouring hills.

The cross, which is rather rudely cut, measures three feet less an inch in height, and across the arms is about one foot eleven inches. In depth the arms are nine inches, on the face which now fronts the garden. The width of the head is thirteen inches, and it rises nine inches above the arms; it is about five inches in thickness close to their upper surface, but grows less towards the top. Below the arms the thickness of the shaft is about seven inches, and its width fifteen inches.

On one face there is an incised cross measuring about ten inches in height by five inches across. It is not placed between the arms, but below them, and is not in the centre of the shaft.

It is probable that in the olden days, the dwellers in this tor-surrounded combe resorted to this cross to offer their devotions, many a prayer doubtless having been breathed, and thanksgiving poured forth before it—

> " This was the scene :—the old man there,
> More motionless than sculptured stone ;
> The moorland beacon wild and bare ;
> And, high upraised in stillest air,
> The cross against the western glare,
> 'Mid glory all its own.
>
> " And, like the seraph strains which flow
> From million harps or golden lyre,
> Such words as these, good angels know,
> Fell from that old man, grave and slow,
> Borne upward through the evening glow,
> As incense, high and higher.
>
> * * *
>
> " ' Thou art 'the same,' for ever One ;
> And Thy Great Sign shall never die,—
> For when the circling years have run,
> A cross no human eye can shun
> Shall e'en out-gleam both star and sun,
> Bright on the eastern sky.' "*

Near the gate of Widecombe churchyard we shall find the base of a cross standing in the centre of the green. The cross itself is gone, and in its place a small yew tree is growing.

---

*T. Vernon Wollaston. *Stat Crux Dum Volvitur Orbis.* Lyra Devoniensis.

This base consists of two steps and is octagonal in shape. A plinth about six inches high runs round the bottom, the sides of it varying from about four feet three inches in length, to a few inches more than this. The sides of the first step measure about four feet long and those of the upper one average about three feet and a half. The steps are each one foot five inches in height, the measurement of the lower one being taken from the top of the plinth, and their edges project a little, after the manner of stairs in carpentry. The tread of the step is about one foot, and the diameter of the top of this basement is about eight feet and a half.

Around the plinth the ground is worn away, exposing the smaller stones which form the foundation of the structure.

Entering the churchyard we shall observe close to the south door of the church, a socket-stone, with the lower part of the shaft of a cross fixed in it. This stone measures three feet six inches by three feet two inches, and at the bottom is quadrangnlar, but its upper edge is roughly formed into an octagon.

The broken shaft is about two feet seven inches in height, and at the top, measures eleven inches by nine and a half. The shape of, it here is octagonal, as, at a short distance from the bottom, which is square, the corners are chamfered.

Built into the exterior of the east wall of the churchyard will be found two parts of a cross, one consisting of a piece of the shaft, and the other of the top of the same with the arms. These pieces are fixed one on the other, but the broken ends do not fit where placed together. Taking the measurement of them as one, I find the height to be three feet four inches, and the distance across the arms is two feet one inch, the depth of them being about ten inches, and the width of the shaft about the same.

The shape of these pieces is octagonal, like the shaft by the church door, but whether they were broken off from that, or are parts of the cross that formerly stood on the basement on the green, cannot, of course, be determined.

We have a good deal of information about matters pertaining to this village in a book entitled *Things New and Old Concerning the Parish of Widecombe-in-the-Moor*, edited by Mr. Dymond, and it is there stated that in January, 1876, in clearing some steps in the church which had formed the ascent to the rood-loft, but which for long years had been hidden from view behind a walled-up Gothic doorway, a piece of the shaft of the churchyard cross was discovered, measuring about twenty inches in length. At the same time three small granite crosses were found, each being twenty-nine inches high, one having an incised cross in the centre, between the arms.

The tower of the church of " Withycombe in the Dartmoores" is justly celebrated for its fine proportions, and the fabric itself has had more written about it than any other of the Dartmoor churches on account of its association with the great thunder-storm of 1638. On a wooden tablet we may read the details of it, in rhyme, said to be written by one Hill, the village schoolmaster, who, it has been supposed, was related to Roger Hill, one of those who perished in the storm.

Our investigations will next lead us to Hameldon, a high and conspicuous hill which forms a barrier between this pleasant combe and the forest. We shall therefore leave the village by the road which leads to the head of the vale, but shall not follow it far. On our left we shall shortly perceive a very steep lane, and making our way up this shall reach a field, across which a path will take us to the commons.

On gaining the summit, we shall find that a wall extends along the lofty ridge, and is carried at one part of its course over a barrow consisting of earth and stone. This barrow is known as Hameldon Beacon, and from this point some landmarks will serve as a guide to enable us to find an old cross which is situated on this hill.

Keeping the wall on our left hand, and proceeding in a direction nearly due north, Two Barrows will soon be reached. Here the wall is carried down the side of the hill towards the west, but we shall continue our course to another barrow, which we shall remark at a short distance off. This is Single Barrow, and from here we shall pass on to Broad Barrow, from the top of which, looking nearly north, we shall see what from here appears like an ordinary granite post, but which we shall presently find to be an ancient cross.

From the Beacon to Broad Barrow we have been able to feast our eyes at every step upon a view embracing the whole of the central parts of the moor, as well as of a number of prominent heights in both the northern and southern portions of it. To anyone wishing to gain some idea of the extent of Dartmoor, Hameldon offers the most advantageous point from which to obtain it, though the true character of the moorland region is not revealed so fully as from Cut Hill in the north quarter of the forest. From the latter height many of the more solitary parts of the great waste are seen, with scarcely a sign of cultivation, while from Hameldon much of the enclosed portion of Dartmoor is commanded, and also a wide extent of South and East Devon. From Cosdon Beacon in the north-north-west, the eye ranges by a vast extent of moor round to Great Mistor in the west, and thence, taking in North Hessary Tor, we look to the south-west, to the dark hills of the southern quarter of the forest, and see in the far distance the Eastern Beacon on Ugborough Moor and near it the neighbouring peak of Brent Hill. Looking across the Widecombe valley we obtain a grand view of numerous rocky eminences, among which are Hey Tor, Rippon Tor and Hound Tor, while nearer to us the noble heights of Honeybag and Chinkwell Tors, and Bonehill Rocks lift their lofty heads above the combe. The view is truly magnificent, and in whichever direction the observer turns he is sure to be impressed with the grandeur of the surroundings, and the wild aspect of the desert range—

> "Where the grey Tor, as in ages of yore,
> Mocks the mad war of the storm on the Moor,
> Bravely exposing its huge granite crest,
> Or wrapt in a cloud like an angel at rest."*

We shall soon reach the old cross which is situated on the hill, just at the point where we sight the house belonging to Headland Warren in the valley below.

We shall find it to be a very rudely-fashioned one, formed out of a slab four feet four inches in height, the width of it immediately below the arms being one foot eight inches. One of the arms—the southerly one—is broken off, and lies on the ground near by. The depth of the remaining one close to the shaft is thirteen inches, but it is not nearly so much as this at its extremity. The head has also been broken, but it does not appear that it ever rose very much above the arms. From the end of the arm which is now remaining,

---

* Capern. *Song of the Devonian.*

to the opposite side of the shaft the distance is two feet two inches. The thickness of this cross at the bottom is eight inches, but it is not much more than six inches higher up. It is leaning considerably towards the west.

On the eastern face are the modern letters H.C., which I take to mean *Hameldon Cross*, and beneath them the letters D. S., while under them again is the date 1854. We shall have observed that on the four barrows, which we have passed on this hill, there were stones set up with the name of each barrow cut on them, and having also the letters D. S., and the same date as we find on the cross. These were placed here to mark the boundary of Natsworthy Manor, at the time it belonged to the Duke of Somerset, and the old cross being also a manor boundary, had the letters engraven on it as well. The original purpose of this cross was doubtless the same as that which it serves at present.

Mr. Spence Bate in his paper to which we have more than once referred,* and which I had not seen when my first account of this cross was published, in 1883, gives the date upon it as 1839, in which year, he says, it was set up after having been for some time partially buried in the soil. There is some confusion here, for the date on the cross is as we have given it. About twenty years ago I met one of the men at Widecombe who was concerned in the cutting of the figures and letters upon it, and also on the other boundary stones.

Bidding adieu to this storm-beaten old stone, standing in loneliness on this lofty hill, we turn southward, and at the distance of two miles and a half shall reach Bittleford Down, where we strike a road that will lead us to the hamlet of Ponsworthy. We turn up the lane on the right and on gaining the open moor, cross the northern edge of Sherberton Common to Dartmeet Hill, which we descend for some distance. A green path leading from the road will be observed just where the latter makes a considerable sweep to the right. This we shall follow, and when about midway down shall reach an object which is known in the neighbourhood as the 'Coffin Stone, and which I have included among the relics we are now examining in consequence of its surface bearing several incised crosses.

---

* *Trans. Plymouth Institut.,* vol. vi.

It is situated immediately beside the path, and consists in reality of two stones, though these were evidently one at some period, having probably been rent asunder, by some convulsion of nature.*

One of the stones—the higher one—has seven small crosses cut on it, and the letters S I, S C, A C, with traces of others. The lower stone has the letters I B, I P, of somewhat larger size, with but two crosses graven on it. The larger of these stones measures eight feet and a half long, by about three feet in width, the other being six feet long and about three and a half feet across at its widest part; this latter is triangular in shape.

The Coffin Stone is so called in consequence of its having long been customary to rest the coffin here, when a corpse is being carried to Widecombe-in-the-Moor for burial. The letters are the initials of some whose remains have here been placed for a while when on the journey to the tomb.† I have seen the mourners grouped around this stone, in the quiet stillness of a summer afternoon, while the bearers rested in their toilsome ascent. The blue sky clear and cloudless, the river below laughing in the sunshine, all nature looking bright and joyous, but failing to cheer those hearts saddened and filled with woe.

We shall obtain a fine view of the vale above Dartmeet from this spot, and shall not fail to admire its beauties. Various kinds of trees fringe the opposite bank of the stream, and with the enclosures of Brimpts form a striking contrast to the rugged steep on this side of the river, where are numerous rude stone remains, scattered among the natural rocks which are thickly strewn around. The hill is crowned with the granite peak of Yar Tor, which towers high above the narrow vale.

We are now on the path which, after tracing across the forest from Walkhampton Common, we left at Dartmeet

---

* Numbers of stones are found In this state on the moor. A superstition connected with them is noticed in an extremely interesting little work, entitled, *Dartmoor and its Borders*, by "Tickler" (Elias Tozer) :— "Our kind guide pointed out a stone, 'rent in twain,' which he said occurred, in all probability, when Jesus was crucified," p. 74.

† Two of those whose names are represented by initials on the stone I knew well. One of them left the moor for the Metropolis, and there some time after I met him. I noticed that the colour was disappearing from his cheek, and in a brief space he returned to Dartmoor to die.

Bridge,* and are thus able to mark its continuance to Widecombe.

Returning to the summit of Dartmeet Hill and retracing our steps over the road, we soon reach a point known as Ouldsbroom Cross, where a road branches to Ashburton. The old stone that formerly marked it, and which has given to the place its name, though no longer on its ancient site, is fortunately not lost. Mr. Dymond first brought it to my notice, and informed me where I should find it. It serves as a gate-post at the entrance to the yard of Town Farm, which is situated just below the church at Leusdon, on the confines of the common, and very nearly two miles from the spot from which it was taken.

I learnt from Mr. Dymond that an old man named William French, who had spent all his life in the vicinity, said that this cross when standing on its original site, was fixed upon as the limit to which the French officers, detained as prisoners of war at Princetown prior to 1815, were permitted to extend their walk on parole of honour.

It would seem from this that the prisoners located at Princetown who were allowed outside the prison walls on parole, were not restricted in their walks to such narrow limits as were those quartered in the various towns in the district, for in the latter case they were not at liberty to go beyond one mile from the town, while this old cross is more than seven miles distant by road from Princetown.

William French gave Mr. Dymond some particulars relative to the removal of Ouldsbroom Cross, and said that it was brought away from its site more than sixty years before, which would be about 1825, by Thomas Hext, at that time the occupier of Town Farm, French then living with him as a parish apprentice. It was conveyed to the farm on a slide drawn by four oxen. The arms were knocked off after its arrival there, on its being found that they interfered with the purpose to which the cross was put.

Passing Ouldsbroom Farm on the Ashburton road, we make our way by Leusdon Church to Town Farm, that we may examine this old cross. We shall notice with regret that the work of Farmer Hext was only too complete. One of the

---

* p. 101, *ante.*

arms has been knocked completely off, while the other only projects about two inches from the shaft, the greater part of it having been broken or chipped off. Holes have also been drilled in it for the reception of hinges. It stands about five feet nine inches above the ground, and is about sixteen inches in breadth immediately below the arms; at the base it is wider.

From Town Farm we make our way to the hamlet of Pound's Gate, and descend to Newbridge, on the Dart. Away on the hill is Holne vicarage, the house in which Charles Kingsley passed his babyhood. Had he remained longer there it is possible that the scenery of the old moor might have exercised a similar influence upon him to that which did the northern coast of the county. From Newbridge we climb the hill, and once more reach the village of Holne, passing through which to Play Cross. we shall turn into the lane that leads to Scoriton. Another long climb and we reach a little common known as Cross Furzes, immediately at the higher end of the valley of Dean Burn, a narrow gorge having steep sides clothed with oak coppices, and through which runs a tributary of the Dart. By the roadside is an old stone about two and a half feet high, and having a letter cut in relief on three of its faces. These are the initials of the names of places to which it points the way, namely, Tavistock, Ashburton and Brent.

A gate in another part ot the little common opens on to Wallaford Down, a breezy tract, whence most extensive views are obtainable, its western slope forming one side of the Dean Burn valley. Across this we might make our way to Dean Church, distant some three miles or more from Cross Furzes, and which from its association with the poet Herrick, who was vicar of the parish for some years before the Commonwealth, and again after the Restoration, will always possess a peculiar interest. Mr. Worthy, in his notice of Dean in the work before referred to, mentions an old head-stone in the churchyard there, having what he supposed were "the massive fragments of the ancient cross" placed round it. The pieces of stone in question have something of the appearance of a broken shaft, but on examination will be found to be portions of an old granite mullion.

Descending the side of Cross Furzes, close to which passed the Abbots' Way as it entered the moor, we cross the stream by a single stone clapper, eleven-and-a-half feet in length, and about three feet wide. This has the date 1705 cut upon it in one place, and in another the letters **B D A**, with the date 1737. Beyond this we pass the ruins of Lambsdown Farmhouse, and after crossing another little stream shall make our way over the common in the direction of Brent Hill, now in full view, and to which we are very near. Soon we shall enter upon a lane, and on arriving at a point where it is crossed by another shall find a directing-stone, standing in a little open space. The letters it bears are not cut in relief like those on the stone at Cross Furzes, but are incised. There are four, and they show the traveller the roads leading to Plympton or Plymouth, Totnes, Ashburton and Tavistock.* Here we strike

---

* The track to Tavistock, the direction of which is indicated on this stone and on the one we have just noticed, was the Abbots' Way, that ancient road, it is thus evident, still being used after the monks were driven from the abbeys with which it communicated. From Broad Rock (p. 72) the branch followed by travellers was in all probability that which led by Plym Steps to Marchants Cross (p. 73), where they would enter upon the road running through Dousland, near which place formerly stood the ancient Yanedone Cross, as mentioned in a previous chapter (p. 68). Having learnt from Mr. Aaron Rowe, of Princetown, that some worked stones were to be seen on Burham Farm, which is not far from Dousland, I have recently visited it in his company, and made an examination of them. One appears to be part of the shaft of a cross, and as it is not far from the holed stone already described (p. 68) there is certainly reason for supposing that one belonged to the other, and that the latter is a true socket-stone. This possible fragment of Yanedone Cross will be found on the right of the lane leading from Dousland to Walkhampton, acting as a post in the gateway of a field belonging to the above-named farm. It is two-and-a-half feet in height and three feet in girth. The corners are cut away, and have a shallow groove sunk in the bevel; the stone is very much worn. Another of the stones forms part of the coping on the wall of the garden in front of the farmhouse, but the most curious are found at the gate in the way leading from there to Walkhampton. One of these, which has not all its sides worked, is three feet high and serves as a post; the other is laid on the top of the hedge and is rather elaborately worked. It measures twenty-two inches by sixteen inches, and is not unlike part of a pedestal. Whether these stones ever helped to form a stepped base of a cross it is impossible to say; they may have formed part of some building near by, or have been brought from the church. The gate-posts of the gardens of some cottages close to the entrance to Town Farm in Walkhampton village, it is plainly to be seen were fashioned for another purpose than that which they now serve.

the ancient track from Ashburton and Buckfast to Plympton, which we have already seen crossing Ugborough moor at Spurrell's Cross, and at other points.* From the latter place eastward to the spot at which we have now arrived, its course was principally over the moor, and though only discernible here and there, I have been able to trace it sufficiently to determine the line it took between the two points. It is interesting as showing the way which the traveller in the old days followed when passing along the southern edge of Dartmoor.

Eastward of Spurrell's Cross the track is plainly to be seen at a ford over the West Glaze, and again near the enclosures of Merrifield Farm, on the edge of Brent Moor. Here, in the formation of a newtake, care was taken not to obstruct the path. The former is detached from the rest of the enclosures, a narrow strip of common being left between, over which the old road runs. A similar arrangement may be seen on Cudlipp Town Down, and in other places, both on the fringe of the waste and in the forest. Not far from this the track leaves the moor, and descends towards the Avon, this part of it being known as Diamond Lane. It is steep, and exceedingly rough, and suitable only as a bridle path; but a tradition existing in the locality speaks of a coach and four horses having once been driven through it. This seems to preserve the recollection of former traffic over it.† The track probably crossed the Avon at a ford somewhere near the present Shipley Bridge, and running over the down by Yolland Farm, where there is still a path, reached the point at which we have now struck it.

But we again leave the old path, and turning into the lane on our right shall cross Gigley Bridge. Skirting Brent Hill, and passing through Lutton we shall descend to the village whence we set out, having thus made the circuit of the moor.

Our examination of these time-worn relics has now terminated, and we shall bid adieu to the wild country in which they stand.

---

* pp. 26, 34, *ante*.

† There is a granite trough in Diamond Lane, overgrown with moss, which the country people suppose to have been made for passing ponies to drink from. But, as there are no means of supplying it with water, this does not seem likely. It was no doubt hollowed out on the spot with the intention of removing it to some farm, and was afterwards abandoned.

For the most part the Dartmoor Crosses, as will have been seen, were erected as marks to the paths which were trodden by travellers in the olden days, and as we pursue these paths now, we are carried back in imagination to the time when over them passed the lordly abbot, the knight with his body-guard of servitors, the merchant journeying with his commodities, or bands of pilgrims bound to the shrine of their patron saint. The grey cross on the heath would serve not only to point out their road, but also to keep them in remembrance of One who gave His life that mankind might not perish. Wynken de Worde in 1496 printed a treatise on the ten commandments, in which occurs the following:—

"For this reason ben Crosses by ye waye, that whan folke passynge see the Crosses, they sholde thynke on Him that deyed on the Cross, and worshyppe Hym above all thynge."

Here was the emblem of his religion standing before the traveller, and bidding him, by the memories it would call forth, cling to it and shun evil. In ancient Egypt figures of Pascht, the avenger of crime, were set up at the junction of roads to remind the people that guilt would be punished; and while these old crosses would tell the same tale, they would also speak of the reward in store for those who "trust in the Lord, and do good" (Psalm xxxvii., 3).

There are many old paths on the moor besides the ones we have here noticed, but with the exception of Cut Lane and the Lich Path, none so interesting as those which led to the four great religious houses on the borders of the southern part of the moor. The paths in its northern division are of a different character; no abbeys were on its verge, and those who passed over its green tracks were chiefly moormen and the settlers in the forest.

The crosses of the moor are, generally speaking, rudely fashioned, and are, without exception, Latin crosses. It is true that a few of them, such as the one near Cadaford Bridge, and Spurrell's Cross, now present the Greek form, but this, is owing simply to the shaft having been broken off and lost. Most of them face east and west, but there are exceptions to this. Siward's Cross is the only one mentioned in any perambulation of the forest, and none but that and Hobajon's Cross are marked on the old map.

The indifference with which our antiquities have been regarded in times past is now happily disappearing, and it is at length recognised that the grey stones of the heath have an interesting story to tell, and one which cannot be lightly passed over by the student of history. There is a charm, too, in antiquarian study, which cannot fail to interest and delight; as a writer in the *Builder* has well said, "Those who have once caught the true flavour of antiquity, and learned what it is to extract its essence of humanity from the heart of an old stone, can very well afford to laugh in turn at those who take it for an axiom that the dying present is infinitely of more value than 'the dead past.'"

The old crosses of the moor are pleasing objects even to the casual passer-by who takes but slight heed of them, but to the antiquary and the student of history, the memories they serve to awaken add to their attractiveness, and endow these weather-stained and rough-hewn stones with a deeper interest and a greater charm.

ADDENDA.

A fine Latin Cross has recently been erected at Cornwood (p. 34). It stands on a stepped base, and forms quite an interesting feature of the village. It bears the date 1902, and the following inscription: "In grateful memory of Frederic Rogers, Lord Blachford, K.C.M.G., and of Georgiana his wife. He served his country faithfully for 25 years in the Colonial Office. Their latter days were spent at Blachford, serving God and doing good to their neighbours." The cross was dedicated by the Bishop of Exeter.

In noticing (p. 35) Cornwood it was stated that Delamore was once the residence of Winthrop Mackworth Praed, the poet. We should have said that it was the seat of William Mackworth Praed, the poet's brother. After the death of his widow Delamore came to his daughter, who had previously married Admiral Parker.

It is satisfactory to note that Widecombe has again its Churchyard Cross. The part built into the wall (p. 166) now surmounts the shaft near the south porch. It stands about six feet high. This good work was done some time since.

Quite recently death has removed the Rev. C. H. Crook, for several years vicar of Sheepstor, and to whom we have had occasion to refer (p. 65).

It is also necessary to mention that Highlands (p. 31) is no longer occupied by Mr. William Coryton, of Pentillie.

I have seen it stated that a modern cross on Cosdon marks the Venville bounds. This is not correct. There is an upright stone there marking the boundary of some mineral rights, but the rights of the Venville tenants extend a considerable distance beyond it. I also find that another writer states that Petre's Cross can be seen from near Huntingdon Cross. This, however, is not so. A stone post on the brow of the hill is seen, but not the broken shaft of the old cross (p. 17).

Having been asked about Bulstone, or Bulhornstone, Cross, near South Brent, it may be well to explain that it is merely a name given to the point where the road from Aish to Bulhornstone Farm and Owley crosses a lane leading up towards Aish Ridge. I could never learn of any stone cross standing there. What has been thought to be the base of one, was really made for a millstone. It was intended for the mill at Owley, but owing to a flaw was never taken there, but was placed in the centre of the cross roads. I gathered these particulars many years ago from an old man who remembered when the stone was cut.

On p. 46, read 'Bidlin; p. 96, set up for upset; p. 103, Stascombe; p. 114, Forstall.

INDEX.

ABBOTS' WAY, The, 18, 19, 21, 26, 66, 67, 70, 71, 72, 73, 79, 84, 88, 103, 105, 150, 172, 173
Addiscott, Cross at, 130
Aish Ridge, 12
Amicia, Countess of Devon, 57
———, Deed of, 57, 60, 75, 77
Ancient Customs, 3
——— Tracks. *See* Tracks.
Antiquarian Study, Charm in, 176
Ashburton, 106 ; Base of Cross at, 106 ; Neighbourhood of, 107

BAGGA'S BUSH, 22 ; Guide Stone near, 22
Balbeny and Pushyll, Track from, 149
Barn Hill, 79
Beatland Corner, 46 ; Base of Cross at, 46
Beckamoor Combe, 79
——— Cross, 79
Beechwood, 40
Beetor Cross, 144, 145 ; Traditions connected with, 145
Belstone Rectory, Inscribed Stone near, 124 ; Village, 124
Bennet's Cross, 145, 146
Bickham, 60
Bickleigh, 46 ; Cross at, 59 ; Church, 59 ; Road blocked, 60 ; Vale, 58
Bidder, George, 143
Bishop's Stone, The, 157
Blachford, 34
Blackabrook, Clapper over, 149
Blackaton Cross, 38 ; Tradition connected with, 38 ; View from, 39
——— Slaggets, 38
Black Down, 114, 115, 116
Blacksmith's Pool, 134
Blackwood Path, The, 72
Blizzard, Death in the, 42
Bloody Pool, 10

Boclond, 75, 76 ; Derivation of the name, 77
Border Crosses, 8 ; Scenery, 4 ; Towns, 2
Boringdon, 45 ; Camp, 45
Boundaries, 13, 15, 16, 20, 22, 75, 146
Bovey Heathfield, Cross formerly on, 160
——— Tracey, Crosses at, 157, *et seq.* ; Church Cross, 159 ; Removal of, 159 ; Inscribed Stones in Churchyard, 160 ; Market Cross, 158 ; Mayor's Monday, 158
Bra Tor, Cross on, 117
Bray, Mrs., 108, 109
———, Rev. E. A., 109, 115, 122
Brent Bridge, 22 ; Fair, 10 ; Hill, 9
——— Moor, Boundary of, 20 ; Crosses marking boundary of, 15 ; Inquisition on boundary of, 15 ; Stones marking boundary of, 22
——— South. *See* South Brent.
——— Tor, Cross formerly at, 115 ; Traditions concerning, 114, 115
Bridges' History of Okehampton, 119, 122
Broad Rock, 72, 73, 173
Brock Hill Mire, 71, 103
Brooke, Sir James, 63, 66
Browney Cross, 45, 46, 57 ; View from, 46
Buckfast Abbey, 77, 105, 106
———, Track to Plympton from, 26, 174
Buckfastleigh Church, 106
——— Churchyard, Cross in, 106
Buckland Abbey, 57, 61
——— in-the-Moor, Cnurch of, 163 ; Crosses at, 163, 164 ; Neighbourhood of, 164

Buckland Ford, 18, 71 ; View from, 19
——— Monachorum Cross, 61, 62 ; Restoration of, 61, 62
——— Monachorum, Inscribed Stones formerly at, 62, 110 ; Pillar in Churchyard, 62 ; School at, 62 ; Track to Buckfast from, 68, 84 ; Village, 61
Bude Lane, 124
Bulhornstone Cross, 178
Burham Farm, Shaft of Cross on, 173
Burrator, 64. 65 ; Reservoir, 65, 85 ; Wood, 51
Bush Meads. 19
Butterdon Hill Stone Row, 13, 15, 28

CADAFORD BRIDGE, 39, 49, 57 ; Cross near, 49 ; Surroundings of, 50
Calisham Down, 54
Cann, George, 130
Carrington, 89, 92
Carwithen, Rev. Charles, 155
Castle Ring, 45
Chagford, Neighbourhood of, 136, 137
——— Church, 137 ; Crosses found in, 137
Chapel Lands, 123
Charter of King John, 3, 78
Childe the Hunter, Death of, 95 ; Legend of, 88, 89, 90
Childe's Tomb, 88 ; Cross formerly on, 94 ; Description of, 91 ; Destruction of, 89 ; Discovery of, 91 ; Inscription on, 89, 93 ; Remains near, 91, 92, 93
Cholera, Deaths from, 43
Cholwich Town, 36 ; Cross at, 36
Coaker, Jonas, 148
———, of Sherburton, 98
Coffin Stone, The, 169, 170
Colebrook, 45 ; Chapel at, 45
Coppard, Rev. W. I., 43, 59
Copriscrosse, 57, 60
Commons of Devon, The, 3
Cornwood, 34, 35 ; Church, 35 ; Crossroads at, 34 ; Cross at, 177
Coryndon Ball Gate, 12
Cosdon, 125, 126, 177
Cranbrook Castle, Inscribed Stone near, 137
Crapstone Farm, Shaft of Cross on, 62, 63
Crazy Well Pool, 85, 86 ; Cross near, 87

Cross, The, 4, 5 ; A bond-mark, 6 ; A burial monument, 6 ; Earlier than the Church, 5 ; Purposes of, 175 ; The centre of village life, 5
——— Furzes, 103 ; Guide Stone at, 172 ; Clapper near, 173
——— Park, 141, 156
——— Roads, 6
Crosses, Destruction of, 5 ; Probable date of, 83 ; Style of those on Dartmoor, 6, 175
Crossing, Mrs. Joseph, 45.
Crucem de Wolewille, 57, 58
——— Siwardi, 57
Cudlipp Town Down, Path on, 174
Cuming, Chas., 141, 164
Cumston Tor, 103
Cut Lane, 149

DARK LAKE. 72
Dartmeet, 101 ; Hill, 169 ; View from, 170
Dartmoor, Antiquities of, 4 ; Aspect of, 2, 3 ; Crosses, 6, 7 ; Elevation of, 2 ; Extent of, 1 ; Old map of, 13, 74, 76 ; Situation of, 2
——— Inn, 117
——— Preservation Association, 96, 97
Dean Burn, Valley of, 71
——— Church, 172
Debben and the Grey Wethers, 147
Delamore, 35, 177
Derges, William, 155
Diamond Lane, 174
Dockwell Gate, 103
Dousland, 68, 173 ; Socket-stone at, 67, 68
Down Ridge, 103 ; Crosses on, 100, 101
Drake, Sir Francis, 61
Drewsteignton, 136
Drift Lane, 149
Dry Lake, 72
——— Lakes, 101
Dunsland Cross, 121
Dunstone, Granite block at, 164
Durdon Cross, 121

EASTERN BEACON, The, 10 ; Track near, 72
Eden, Richard, 93
Elfordleigh, 45
Elfords, The, 65, 66

Elsford, Cross at, 140
Emmett's Post, 39
Erme, The, 30, 72
────── Pound, 72
Evans, Rachel, 109, 111

FARDLE, 34
────── Stone, The, 32, 33
Feather Tor, 79
Fice's Well. *See* Fitz's Well.
Fingle Gorge, 137; Track to, 141
Firestone Ley, 131
Fitz, John, 121, 122
Fitzford, Conduit at, 122
Fitz's Well, near Okehampton, 121; Cross at, 121, 122, 123; Tradition concerning, 121, 122; View from, 123
──────, near Princetown, 121, 122, 149, 150
Forstall Cross, 114
Fox and Hounds Inn, 117
Fox Tor, 88
────── Mire, 88, 95
────── Newtake, 96; Cross in, 96; Head of Cross in, 94, 96, 97
French, William, 171

GAVESTON on Dartmoor, 86
Gidleigh, 133
Gigley Bridge, Guide Stone near, 173
Glaze, The, 22
Gloves at Fairs, 10, 115
Goodameavy, 56
Goodamoor, 40
Gratton Farm, Inscribed Stone at, 54
Green Hill, 71
Greenwell Down, 54
Greenwell Girt, 55; Base of Cross near, 55
Grey Wethers, 147
Guide Stones, 22, 115, 116, 119, 144, 146, 150, 151, 172, 173
Gudula, St., 107
Gulval, St., 107
Gulwell, Cross at, 107

HALSTOCK FARM, 123
Hameldon, 167, 168; Cross on, 168, 169; View from, 168
Hanger Down, 34
Hapstead Ford, 103
Harford Bridge, Erme, 30

Harford Bridge, Tavy, 111
────── Church, 28
────── and Ugborough Moors, Boundary between, 13
Harvey, Wm. Phillips, 142
Hawns and Dendles, 35
Hawson Gate, Cross near, 105
Heath Stone, 146
Headless Cross, 141
Hele Cross, 154; Tradition connected with, 154
──── Moors, 144
Hembury Castle, 105
Hemerdon, 40
Herring, Rev. Edmond, 69
Hexworthy, 99, 100, 102
High Down, 117
Higher Atway, Cross at, 158
────── Coombe, Cross at, 156
Highlands, 31, 177
Hisworthy Tor, North, 79
Hobajon's Cross, 12, 14, 15, 74
Holne Churchyard, Cross in, 104; Curious epitaph in, 104
────── Moor, 103
Holy Street, Cross at, 134, 135
Hookmoor Cross, 23. 24
Horn's Cross, 102, 103; Track near, 103
Horrabridge, Incised cross at, 63
Horse Ford, 101, 102
Horse Pit Cross, 152
Howard, Nathaniel, 58
Huccaby, 101
Huckworthy Bridge, 69; Cross on Common near, 69
Huntingdon Corner, Lower, 20
────── Cross, 20, 71; Surroundings of, 21
────── Warren, 19; Bridge at, 19, 146

ILSINGTON, 161
Inga Tor, 69
Inscribed Stones, 15, 32, 54, 62, 63, 68, 109, 119, 124, 125, 137, 157, 160
Ivybridge, 29, *et seq.*; Bridge at, 29, 30; Church, 31; Road to Tavistock from, 31

JELLINGER, Christopher, 11
Jobber, 66
Jobbers' Cross, 79
Jobbers' Path, 66
Jockey Down's House, 118
Johns, Rev. John, 86
Jones, Rev. J. P., 94, 153

KEMPE, A. J., 109
Kempthorn, Sir John, 25
King, R. J., 106
King Way, The, 116
Kingsley, Charles, 104, 172

LADWELL ORCHARD, 106
Lady Littler, 106
Lake, 117
Lambsdown Farm, 71, 173
Lane, Mrs. Bridget, 104
Lawe, Rev. G. L. G., 133
Lee Moor tramroad, 45
Leeper, Cross at, 151
Leigh Steps, 134
Lether Tor, 51, 85 ; Bridge, 85
Lich Path, 114, 149
Long Ash Hill, 150 ; Guide Posts near, 150 ; Menhir on, 80
Longtimber Tor, 113
Lower Whiteyborough, 58
Lowery, 84
Lukesland, 28
Lustleigh, 157 ; Inscribed Stone at, 157
———— Cleave, 155
Luxmore, Miss, 121
Lydford, 115 ; Circular Stone at, 116 ; Churchyard, 116 ; Gorge, 115 ; Guide Stone at, 115
Lydia Bridge, 12
Lynch Down, 50 ; View from, 64
Lynscott, Cross at, 140, 141, 164

MAGGIE CROSS, 148
Mainstone Wood, 58 ; Cross, 58
Mallock. Rawlin, 162
Manaton, 154 ; Cross formerly at, 154 ; Disappearance of, 155, Socket-stone at, 155.
Mann, William, 103
Map of Dartmoor, Ancient, 13, 74, 76
Marchants Bridge, 52
———— Cross, 50, 51, 63, 66, 67, 73, 173 ; View from, 51
Mardle, The, 103
Maristowe, 60
Mary Tavy Churchyard, 114 ; Cross in. 113, 114
Maximajor Stone, 141
Maynstoncrossa, 57
Meavy, 52, et seq.: Churchyard, 54 ; Cross at, 52, 53 ; Restoration of, 53
———— Oak, 52
Meldon, 119
Meripit Hill, Cross formerly on, 148

Merivale Bridge, 79, 80
Merrifield Farm, Track at, 174
Mew, The, 87
Middlecott, 139
Milton, Stones at, 62
Monkeys' Castle. 81
Moon's Cross, 128
Moor Gate, 151
Moortown, 80
Moretonhampstead, 141 ; Cross at, 141, 142, 143 ; Cross Tree at, 141, 142
Murchington, Cross formerly at, 134

NEWCOMBE, JOHN. 74
Newhouse. See Warren House Inn
Newhouse, near Rippon Tor, 163
Newleycombe Lake, 87
Newnham, 45
Niel Gate, 46
North Bovey, 152 ; Cross, 153
———— Lew Cross, 120
Nun's Cross, 73 ; Derivation of name, 78

OCKMENT, EAST, 124
Ogham Alphabet, 33
———— Characters. Inscriptions in, 110, 111
Okehampton Castle, 119, 123
————————, Cross formerly at, 119 ; Park, 121 ; Stone in Church Wall, 119, 120
Old Newnham, 40
Older Bridge, 88
Orchard, John, 126
Ouldsbroom Cross, 171
Owen's Book on the Roads, 146 et seq.
Owley Gate, 25
Oxen employed, 98
Oxenham, 129 ; Cross, 129 ; Tradition of White Bird, 129

PAYNE'S BRIDGE, 132
Peat Track to Hook Lake, 26
———— Works, 17
Peter Tavy, Remains of Cross at, 111, 112 ; Churchyard, 112
Perambulations of Forest, 3
Petre's Cross, 17 ; Mutilation of, 17, 177
Petre, Sir William, 18
Phillips, of Lee Moor, 37
Potsans Bridge, 32

Play Cross, 105
Plym, Ford near source of the, 73
—— Steps, 72, 173
Plymouth Municipal Records, 151
Plympton, 41, *et seq.*; Castle, 41, 42 ; Church of St. Mary, 43 ; Church of St. Maurice, 41 ; Cross at, 40, 41 ; Grammar School, 42 ; Guildhall. 42 ; House, 42 ; Priory, 43 ; Track to Sampford Spiney from, 43, 44 ; Track to Tavistock from, 82.
Prewley Moor, 118
Prideaux, John, 25, 28
Pu Tor, 69, 70
Puckie Stone, 134
Purl's Cross. *See* Spurrell's Cross

QUEEN VICTORIA'S CROSS, 102

RED LAKE FORD, 71
Ringhole Copse, Cross at, 130
Ringleshutt's Mine, 103
Rippon Tor, Cross on, 161, 162
Roborough Down. 60, 62, 63
Roborough, Holed Stone near, 59, 60
Rock Hotel, The, 63
Rogers' School, Dame Hannah. 32
Roman Camp, The, 38
Roman's Cross, 37
Rowe, Rev. Samuel, 42
Rundle Stone, The, 150

ST. JOHN'S HERMITAGE, Cross formerly at, 109
St. Leonard's Well, 65
St. Mary's Chapel, 126
Saddle Bridge, 101
Sampford Spiney, 70 ; Cross at, 70
Sand Parks, 88
Sandowl Cross, 23, 25
Sanduck, Cross at, 160
Sandy Way, 95, 103
Shaden Brake, Cross at, 48
Shady Combe, 55
Sharp Tor, Inscribed Stone near, 15, 16
Shaugh Bridge, 48 ; Church, 47 ; Cross, 47
Sheeps Tor, 66 ; Sheepstor, 85, 177; Base of Cross at, 64 ; Church, 65, 66 ; Church House, 66 ; Cross, 64, 65 ; Stone post at, 66 ; Track to, 64 ; Village, 64
Shipley Peat Works, 17

Shorter Cross, 139
Siward. 77
Siward's Cross, 73. 77, 78, 88, 105 ; Derivation of name, 77 ; Dimensions of, 73, 74 ; Inscription on, 74, 75, 76, 77
Skir Ford, 100 ; Gert, 99
Skits Bridge, Stone near, 116
Smalacumbacrosse, 57, 63
Smalacumbalak, 63
Smith, Rev. Merton, Memorial Cross to, 43
—— Samuel, 100
Snowdon Hole, 103
Sourton 118 ; Base of Cross at, 118
—— Down, Cross on, 118 ; Inscription on, 118, 119
South Brent Church, 11 ; Cross, 11
—— Harton Farm, Cross at, 153, 156
——Tawton, 128 ; Quarries, 129
——— Zeal, 126 ; Cross at, 127 ; Tradition relating to, 127, 128
Southerleigh, 117
Southmead House, Base of, Cross at, 135
—— —— Mr., 135
Spurrell's Cross, 26, 27, 40, 72, 174 ; Stone row near, 27 ; View from, 27
Stanbury, John, 127
Stannaburrows, 100
Stascombe Telling-place, 103
Stephens, Dr. W. J., 140, 164
Stevens' Grave, 113
Sticklepath, 125 ; Inscribed Stone at, 125
Stittleford's Cross, 162
Stone Adze, 25
—— Cross, 136, 137
—— Park, 107
—— Rows, 13, 15, 27
Stones, Inscribed. *See* Inscribed Stones
—— Cloven, 170
Stony Bottom, 72
Stowford Cleave, 30
Streams, Principal, 2
Stumpy Cross, 137
Swincombe, The, 78 ; Stone pillar near Upper Valley of, 73, 78

TAVISTOCK, 83, 108 ; Abbey, 111 ; Cross formerly at, 108 ; Inscribed Stones at, 109, 110 ; Track from Moreton to, 149 ; Worthies, 83.